The Relieved Widow
Unexpected Truths of Suicide Loss

Amanda-Lee Pitzer

BLUE HAT
PUBLISHING
BOISE · KNOXVILLE · NASHVILLE · SEATTLE
WWW.BLUEHATPUBLISHING.COM

First Print Edition, 2024

Printed in China

Publishing Services: Jodi Cowles, Brandon Janous, and Rachael Mitchell (Blue Hat Publishing)

Cover Design: Rachael Mitchell (Blue Hat Publishing)

Interior Layout: Jodi Cowles (Blue Hat Publishing)

ISBN (print): 978-1-962674-18-8

ISBN (ebook): 978-1-962674-19-5

Contents

Dedication

This is for anyone who ever found themselves drowning, living a life they had not imagined for themselves. I hope that through my story you find hope, courage, and restoration.

Part One: Swept Out to Sea

Prologue

One summer, I spent most of my time with a friend who had a pool membership. This was *huge* for me as I grew up during a recession where my dad had lost his job; spending money on a membership just wasn't feasible. So, every day we were together that summer, we spent at the pool. What was unique about this pool, however, was the high-dive board. I had never seen one of these in person and used to watch people jump off it in absolute awe. They would make an extravagant splash and stay under for what seemed like forever. Eventually, they would explode back up, breaking the surface with loud gasps for air.

Every day we swam, ate lunch, and lounged on the pool deck and every day I would marvel at the bravery of those who climbed up those stairs. They seemed to do it without any trepidation, and I was terrified to try. Eventually, my friend worked up the nerve to do the high dive. She teased me endlessly for not trying, and eventually as the summer drew to a close, I made my way toward that ladder.

My heart was pounding as I walked over, worried that everyone was looking at me. I climbed so much slower than most, and perhaps the only reason I kept going was because I had no choice. There were others climbing up behind me; it was now expected. I remember getting to the top and gripping the rails, terrified – it was so much scarier than I had envisioned. I felt a mix of wanting to faint, wanting to throw up, and just wanting to get it over with. I let several people come up and go ahead of me as I stood there in an absolute panic. I couldn't just back down the ladder now. How humiliating would that be?

My friend began to yell at me from the pool deck, a mix of taunting and cheering me on. Finally, without any grace or fanfare, I walked towards the end of the diving board. Before I knew it, I did a straight pencil jump off the diving board, the tummy feeling in full effect as I raced towards the water. I knew right away this was a terrible idea as I plunged beneath the water. I had been holding my breath for so long already – I knew I needed to breathe – but I was in so deep. I kicked and kicked, trying to get up to the surface faster, but I felt like I was standing still. I stared up through the water as the bubbles raced up past me, feeling like I was so close but so far from the breath I needed.

Finally, I broke the surface with the most dramatic sound as I gasped for air. I stayed there, treading water and breathing deeply as I processed what had just happened. I was almost in shock. Finally, I lazily swam to the ladder and shakily climbed out of the pool. I looked back, still catching my breath, marveling at what I survived.

The night of my husband's funeral there I was again, still in shock and out of breath, realizing that I had just escaped the hell I had been living in for so long.

One

Suddenly a Widow

I hadn't slept well all night, and when I looked over at the clock and saw it was five a.m., I took it as a good excuse to get out of bed and away from him. Before I finally fell asleep the night before he had told me, "You know I'll never be able to see you with someone else." I couldn't believe he had the audacity to say that after all of his years of cheating. The night before he had even told me, "I need you to hate me." Well, mission accomplished. After last night's confession, I knew his issues were so much more than cheating, and I had no choice but to leave him for the sake of our kids. I couldn't stay married to him once he decided to fill me in on his past.

I slowly peeled back the covers, grabbed my robe, and slid sideways out of bed, pausing occasionally if I thought I heard him stir. I tiptoed to the door, opened it slowly, and made it quietly downstairs. I sat on my spot on the couch, and while I would have normally made coffee, I was still reeling from the day before. I began to replay each moment of the previous day and all of its revelations in my mind. As I did this, I began to go further back, slowly connecting the dots over the years. Finally seeing all the lies for what they were, and yet realizing there was more afoot than met the eye. I sat there in stunned silence until I wasn't even sure how to pray. I knew he needed help that he wasn't getting, and I decided I was going to need to seek help on his behalf that day. I was just waiting for his therapist's office to open at nine a.m. so I could find out what I should do.

Finally, I grabbed the devotional I had begun working through about six weeks prior. My friend had recommended it, and seeing as she was in a very similar situation, I began to read and meditate on each word. *The Circle Maker: Praying Circles Around Your Biggest Dreams and Biggest Fears* had become a daily part of my life during what had become the darkest time that I had ever walked through. The premise of the book was that you were to stay in prayer until God answered, circling around the issue with prayer over and over and over again.

I was spending considerable time praying over my husband and our marriage, praying for him to quite literally come to Jesus and be the man my kids and I needed. However, I realized as I worked through the book that God was speaking to me and pointing me in other directions. I felt distinctly in my soul that God was telling me I needed to begin to pray for a future. Specifically for the house I lived in, the friends in my neighborhood, and safety. I was also told to stop praying for who I wanted my husband to become and instead pray over the husband I deserved to have.

When I first felt God prodding me about the house, I thought it was because we were currently in a lawsuit with the developer of our home. I took this to mean, "Okay, we are winning this suit, and then we are moving!" I began looking at real estate in the area, dreaming of somewhere our family could start over. It was then, as I began to pray over our home, that He directed me to pray for the types of neighbors and friends that we wanted. I remember very specifically praying over the types of friends that we needed in our lives. Then, I remember Him directing me to pray for our safety. I wasn't sure about this at all, but briefly did as I was told and then went back to planning where we might move next. I had no idea that my ideas of what God was trying to tell me were so vastly different from what he had in store for us.

As I picked up my book, I flipped to the next page and tried to focus on the words. It was difficult because I was feeling so incredibly broken and worn out. I was too tired to pray. I was overwhelmed by my lack of understanding of what had really been going on. The next thing I knew, I heard my husband coming downstairs, so I quickly flipped my book shut and turned on the TV. He came up behind me and asked, "What are you doing?" I motioned to the TV. I couldn't even talk to him. I tried to mumble something to go along with my hand gesture but fell short. He then went back upstairs. I heard some doors opening and closing, and I assumed it was the boys waking up and making their way to the playroom. Silence fell back over the house again.

I'm not sure how much longer I sat there, but I heard a loud BANG pierce the quiet. I immediately jumped up and told myself one of the boys was in the hallway and had dropped something. I flipped on the light and looked up the stairs but saw no one, just closed doors. I knew at that moment what had happened. I ran up the stairs and went to open our bedroom door, only to find it locked. I banged on it and called his name. I remember calling out, "No, No, No!" I then remembered that there was a key to the bedroom doors sitting atop one of the doorframes. It had been sitting there since we moved in two years prior, never having needed to touch it. I raced downstairs and jumped over and over until I finally was able to touch it enough to send it falling to the floor. I located it and went racing back up the stairs.

I struggled to get the little key into the hole and find the right spot to pop the lock. At last, it popped, and I was able to fling the door open. The room was dark, and I heard nothing. I reached in to flip the light switch and was met with a hazy room where I saw my husband sitting up in bed, bloody and moving his mouth. I immediately slammed the door shut, and it was at that moment my boys came out of the playroom wanting to know why I was screaming Daddy's name. I still don't remember doing this. I demanded that the boys immediately go downstairs; I told them Daddy was hurt, and I needed to get him help, so they were going to the neighbors. Somehow, I also put the dogs into the boy's playroom as we left the house.

It was six a.m. the day after Christmas, and nobody was awake. I banged on three neighbors' doors in the freezing cold, all of us barefoot, waiting for someone to take my eight and nine-year-old, who were clad in their Christmas pajamas so they would not have to see or hear anything else. I was on the phone with 911, telling them I had to make sure the kids were somewhere first. They were on the phone with me as I kept telling my kids we were going to be okay over and over. After what seemed like forever, someone opened the door, and I practically threw them inside. I told them there was an emergency and I would be back and ran back towards the house.

As I ran back, the operator began to ask me questions, "Was I sure he was gone? How did I know?" Thinking back to his moving lips, I said I would go back to the bedroom and check. With the operator in my ear, I opened the bedroom door. This time, I wasn't just met with haze, but I was instead met with what felt like a physical punch to the face as the smell of gunpowder hit my senses. I remember physically reacting and jerking my head back as if I had been hit by the smell. I looked at my husband, and now, seeing that the color was missing from his face, I knew he was gone, and there was nothing to be done. I collapsed in the hallway with the operator coaching me through a tragic scenario. He somehow helped me get back downstairs and to the couch as he talked to me while I waited for help. He told me how well I did. Over and over, he told me how this was awful but that I made sure to put my kids first and protect them from any further damage. Yes, they had just lost their father, but I had spared them seeing his body, smelling the gun, or seeing the house filled with officers and their crackling radios. I would forget this part of the conversation for months, as I just remember sitting on the couch as an officer finally arrived and found me. I simply pointed upstairs.

Finally, he came back downstairs and sat next to me. I didn't look at him. I was looking straight ahead in shock. He put his hand slowly on my shoulder and told me that my husband was, indeed, dead. The house filled with more officers, and a female officer took the place beside me and held my hand while I told them what happened that morning. Somehow, they found out that I attended church – maybe I told them? A new detective was sent over as he was also the chaplain for the department. He was amazing, and I thought nothing of it as we sat at the table and he held my hand and took notes at the same time. By this time, my parents had arrived, and as I began to detail more of what led to this moment – the affairs, the threats from *her* husband, the STDs, the abuse, the paranoia

– my mom and dad had to hear all of this news at once. Only one person knew about the man he really was. I had kept it all locked up for so long, afraid and ashamed of what my marriage truly was. It was only now, as I began to step out of it and describe it to someone else - that I finally began to see it for what it was.

At some point, my mom went to the neighbors, collected the boys, and took them to her house. I was desperate to get to them, knowing that their little hearts and minds were confused. I had no idea if they had been watching from the neighbor's windows as our street filled with flashing lights. I wasn't sure if they were being shielded or how long I was even away from them. All I knew was that I needed to get to them and hold them. Truth be told, I think I needed them to hold me. I sat there at the table as I watched my mom drive by with the boys and was taken back to reality. A female officer handed me an overnight bag full of clothes that she had retrieved from my bedroom – because I certainly could not go back in there.

Finally, I was told that the coroner was on the way, and all the questions were over. The detective suggested I leave before they had to remove the body. The body. What a term for my husband. I got up from the chair and almost began to fall. My body could not support the weight of the events of that morning, and it wasn't over yet. I walked to my dad's car, seeing swarms of officers as well as prying eyes from the houses around me. Shamefully, I walked to the car, feeling the weight of the whispers I could not hear. Once inside the safety of the car, I immediately called my good friend and marriage therapist. I blurted out, "I will be with the boys in thirty minutes. I can't go into details, but my husband killed himself, and I have to go tell the boys." Talk about a way to answer the phone. He let out a deep sigh and thought a minute. He told me he was going to call someone well-versed in tragedy, get their opinion, and call me back so that I was as prepared as I could be.

"Amanda-Lee, I'm so sorry," he said, "but none of you are alone. I'm in Pennsylvania, but I'm heading there now." Even now, I can't believe he up and left his family Christmas vacation to be with us.

I hung up the phone, counting the minutes until I would see my babies. Without proper words to say at that moment, I asked my dad if my husband would be in heaven. I knew there were some opinions that suicide is a sin and prevents entry into heaven. I looked at him and saw how much pain was on his face. He sighed and reminded me that people who die by suicide are sick. In fact, they are so sick that they cannot think clearly. Illness, he said, does not prevent people from heaven. Only their own rejection of God can.

I told my dad the previous day, as my husband told me everything he had done wrong, and I had asked him at what point he would turn his life over and seek out forgiveness from the only One who could give it – because at that moment I could not. He knelt next to me and asked for just that – forgiveness – and prayed that he would not "pass this on to my boys." I wasn't sure what he meant at the time, but I had to believe he was truly remorseful and was able to get himself right before he died.

Finally, my phone rang, and I was told to stick with, "Daddy hurt himself, and I called 911 for help. They were not able to save him, and Daddy died." At that moment, my friend, the counselor, said they did not need details. It was best to try to protect them as much as I could but be clear to express that their dad had died. How in the world could I protect them from this? I began to worry about the damage this would do to them, but then, as we pulled up, I had to push that thought aside.

I hardly waited until the car stopped moving as I threw the car door open to get to them. I ran to the front door and was opening it as they pulled it open, crashing into me with cries of, "Mommy! What happened? Where's Daddy?" After a moment of holding them on the porch, I told them we needed to go talk, and I headed straight for my parents' bedroom – the place where I always found comfort as a child. We crawled right into the middle of the bed, and I took one on each side of me, wrapping them as close as I could. I told them exactly what I was told to say. "NO!" is all I remember hearing as they erupted into tears and buried themselves into me as we all cried together.

I'm not sure how much time passed, but my oldest told me he was going to go get some sleep. I went to object, but my mom interjected with, "It's okay, he needs it." He crawled off the bed, down the hallway, and across the house to his room upstairs. I felt as though part of me had been ripped away; he didn't know how much I needed him. I stayed with my youngest, who had just turned eight a few days before, as he began to ask some questions that I tried to answer as best as I could. After a while, he too decided that he needed to get up and go to his room. Then, it was my mom's turn to sit down and hold me in her bed like she had so many times before.

While the boys were resting, I paced the house, not sure what to do. I knew I needed to call his family, but I couldn't wrap my mind around it. After more debating, I went outside and dialed his brother. He worked from home, and for that, I was grateful. I would have hated to have to tell him at work, needing to drive home, and going to his parents' houses. I'm sure he thought it was odd that I was calling him. I never called him. In fact, it was only the day before that his number was put into my phone, "just in case." Now I knew why. Nearly fifteen years of marriage, and I never had my brother-in-law's number. After I was able to get out that he had died at his own hands that morning, it was quiet. I heard my brother-in-law let out a breath, followed by some variation of, "I can't say I'm surprised."

Already in shock, I didn't think I could be surprised by anything. But that admission knocked the wind out of me. It was then that I found out he had struggled with mental health issues as a young adult, finally culminating in joining the military to leave it all behind. Because they had seen his instability years before, it was something they had feared for a long time. But of course, no one told me. Perhaps I would have seen things differently. He told me he would take care of telling his parents, and they would get to us as soon as they could.

Next up on my list of phone calls was my best friend, the only one who knew the truth about the person I had been dealing with. She immediately dropped everything and rushed to my side. When I saw her, the floodgates opened, and I was able to really cry, not for my kids or for his family, but for me. The guilt that was beginning to pile up on me was immeasurable.

Music has always been a big deal for me. For a long time, I kept a journal of lyrics to songs that spoke to me or I found moving in some way. I was never one to journal my feelings, but instead I found connections with other people's words. When I first met my husband, he discovered this passion of mine and I found him one day flipping through these journals. I realize now that I stopped doing this because of what I see now as an invasion of my privacy. But invasion or not, he knew what music meant to me. This forgotten past-time resurfaced a few weeks prior to his death; he had begun screaming at me because I was singing along to a song on the radio. It was a song about a guy telling a girl to come see him when she breaks up with her boyfriend because he would be waiting for her.

He began to accuse me of wanting to be with someone else. There I was, making Christmas cookies, being accused of ridiculous things. He grabbed his keys, slammed the door, and I heard the car start. I remember telling my friend about this the next day, and I told her, "When he left, I was so relieved. I was praying he'd never come back." The weight of those words slammed into me when I saw her. She knew my thoughts and my feelings. All my secrets she held without judgement. She wrapped her arms around me and held me, and I felt safe for the first time in years. There I was, that little girl at the pool again, desperately needing to surface but unable to make my way to the top.

I heard my oldest stirring, so I went upstairs to check on him. He sat up in bed and was quiet for a minute and then told me, "I needed that." I sat with him and we talked a little. I told him I had called his uncle and that he and his grandparents were on the way. He didn't ask any questions about how his dad died, and for that I was so grateful. Instead, he decided to ask me if I would get married again. How he was thinking about that was beyond me. I told him I couldn't think about anything more than one day at a time. I told him I would need to find us a place to live before I could handle much more than that.

He shook his head and said, "I'm just so worried you'll never be happy again. I just want us happy, and right now I don't know if we will be." My poor boy, so deep in shock and grief and carrying the weight of things he should not have to carry. It wrecked my heart. I promised him we would be happy because I knew that was what Daddy wanted. And given our conversations the day before he died, I knew that it was true. To him, his death was our out; our chance for what he knew we deserved to have.

Two

Secrets and Lies

For so many grappling with suicide loss, the actual loss is just the tip of the iceberg. While I had been let in on many of his dark secrets the day before my husband passed, there was still so much that I didn't know and would continue to uncover in the weeks and months to come. A hard drive of evidence of his torrid affairs was left behind for me to find, and I discovered it had been traveling with him in his book bag for weeks. As I talked to others who knew him, I realized they had all been keeping small secrets for him for some time, and I was just beginning to unravel them.

These secrets further complicated my emotions and compounded my shock as I began to see my husband for who he really was. Eventually, there were no more secrets left for me to find, and I began the process of assimilating all of the information into something I could somewhat understand. As I shifted into my role at Tragedy Assistance Programs for Survivors (TAPS) and began to work with newly suicided widows, I found that I was on the receiving end of calls, texts, and emails from women who were coming face-to-face with newly discovered secrets of their spouse as well. For about half of them, they were completely blindsided by the hidden debt, addictions, affairs, and other indiscretions that they had no idea existed until that moment. They were reeling from loss as well as discovering that the person they had shared a life with was a fraud.

I understood to a point, but because my husband had largely come clean, even just hours before his death, I couldn't imagine being completely and utterly in the dark, with nowhere to hurl my anger, hurt, and confusion. Not that I had done any of that myself; I was in too much shock. But as the weeks and months wore on, I found myself needing to ask so many questions. But at least I had some understanding of his mental state when he passed. For others who find out after the fact, and sometimes by accident, it only sets back the ability to process and understand the loss. Some of these secrets are so severe that it puts all decisions on hold as basic needs like housing have to be quickly decided when the financials are suddenly called into question. Some will lose their homes due to debt; some have discovered their things were willed to someone else, and others discover that there was even another child they were unaware of. Everyone has secrets, but oftentimes those who are mentally afflicted carry many more than we could have ever imagined, which is compounded by their inconceivable death.

I know for myself I kept a lot of secrets hidden as a means of protecting him. I wanted to try to preserve what others thought about him as long as I could. But as I carried those extra burdens, it only served to make me suffer as I walked this path alone. Along with the weight of the secrets, it kept me stuck in a vicious cycle of anger toward him and regret for not knowing (or pretending not to know) what had been going on all along. Even as I tried, I found so many people knew at least some of his secret life and therefore, I no longer had to carry it alone. Even if they didn't know everything, even their "feelings" that there were things going on that shouldn't have been were enough to let me know that I could stop wasting my energy protecting his memory. I finally came to the realization that I had to stop lying to myself and everyone else about who he was.

It is unimaginable to be faced with the fact that your spouse could be guilty of such dishonesty and duality, especially when you loved that person despite their shortcomings. But it is important to remember that this information does not say anything about who you are. You are still the same person, and their secrets have nothing to do with you. It is very common to wonder if we could have done better or been better to avoid this, but the burden is not yours to bear. You are not responsible for their secrets or lies. Even if you said or did something to directly or indirectly communicate that you would not tolerate, or participate in, or allow certain things...the blame still rests with the person who made the choice to hide or conceal.

The anger and even rage you may feel upon discovery is normal and to be expected. Without being able to confront and question the reasons for their actions, you can often feel that you are lacking closure in the wake of unanswered questions. How do you move past something so hurtful when you feel not only loss - but anger, doubt, and confusion? For me, two things helped. Over time, as I was able to understand that my husband had suffered from mental illness for years, I began to see that I was not the cause of his behavior. Being able to understand that it was not my fault allowed me to begin to let it go. I was still deeply hurt, but with therapy and this new understanding, I was able to forgive myself for not knowing, for ignoring it, and finally, for feeling humiliated that my husband could do this to us. Once I worked through this, the anger began to fade until, instead of being angry, I felt so heartbroken as I finally understood what a broken man he was.

Three

Trying to Understand

As time moved on, I found myself going about my day when a thought or a memory would slam into me like a freight train. I would rewatch a scene play out like a movie in front of me from a new perspective. When the film ran out, I would find a puzzle piece on the floor. This happened repeatedly for a few years. These puzzle pieces became corners, edges, and small pieces of a much larger picture that I could not see before. While I doubt, I will ever collect all of the pieces, I now have enough of the puzzle to begin to understand, at least in part, what was going on in our fifteen years of marriage. Even in the early years, when we didn't seem to have any alarming red flags, I can see the beginnings of their development so clearly now.

When I received the casualty report from the military, it was the first time I saw the phrase "mental unsoundness" as an underlying cause of death. Clearly, there was an acknowledgment that even though he had never received an official mental health diagnosis, the understanding was the same. His mental health had deteriorated to the point where he was in agonizing pain and needed it to end. As I read and re-read these words, I just didn't understand how he could get to this point. I had no idea the battle that he was fighting every second of every day. I thought he was the problem, or I was the problem, or his behavior was the problem. I was unaware that the behavior was merely a symptom of something much deeper.

I can't explain it, but so many times, I would walk into a room and just get this feeling that something was wrong. I would study him, try to talk to him about something small, and just know something had changed. Finally, ever so delicately, I would ask him what was wrong, and I never knew what type of reaction I would get. I would ask him because so many times, I just knew that I had done something wrong to upset him. But his answer, most of the time when I sensed whatever this shift was, remained, "I don't know."

I heard it so many times, and every time, it was unnerving. How do you not know what is wrong, and perhaps more importantly, how was there such a shift that I could sense the energy around him changing? Sometimes this was scarier than when he was screaming or breaking things. On more than one occasion, I would try to suggest that he get some help. Talk to someone. Someone that wasn't me, the enemy.

The hang in his head and the slope in his shoulders were screaming that there was a far deeper problem than stress. He would insist that no one could help, that therapy wasn't for him, or that if I just left him alone, he'd be fine. Sometimes, hours later or the next morning, he would be fine. He would demonstrate these mood swings over the years with varying severity and frequency. I always brushed it off as a type of stress that I would never understand. While I may have been a military spouse, I would never be a military member. He reminded me often that I would never know, and try as I might to get him to tell me about his days at work, he refused.

These mood swings would develop into full-fledged depression when he deployed. Months of emails with not a positive thing to say, and when I tried to share what was happening at home, it seemed to make it worse. I was never sure what to share or what to hide because instead of highs and lows in his mood, there were only lows or anger. Again, I would tell him to seek help, even if it was with the chaplain, to keep it "off the books," but it was always out of the question. But then, homecoming would near, and the excitement in his voice would return, and we would have beautiful homecomings. The happiness would last about a week, and then he would start to show those mood swings that he told me he didn't understand.

Over time, he coped with these feelings and fell into addiction, as many with mental health issues do. But instead of drugs or alcohol or other substances, his drug of choice was sex. He stopped hiding his affinity for porn, and I soon discovered that there was a very real addiction. As with most drugs, the mild stuff no longer did it for him. He tried to bring this to the bedroom and was met with my rejection. The hard line in the sand that I drew for him became his perceived permission to seek it out elsewhere. He began to threaten me with doing this if I didn't comply with his many requests. At one point, I began to wish he would so he would just leave me alone. His anger for me began to sit at a constant slow simmer.

He was transferred around this time to a base in another state, but since I had just started a brand-new job, I convinced him that the boys and I should stay behind. It was only two years, and he would come home every other month. It wasn't just my job keeping me put; I was not moving away from all that I knew to live somewhere where I would be isolated and alone with him. It wasn't easy to convince him to stay behind, but he finally decided keeping me employed was better for everyone. He also realized he had freedom and didn't have to hide who he was anymore.

The distance at first was good for us. The constant fighting was gone, I didn't have to see his mood swings, and I felt some relief. He even seemed kinder and gentler. The distance seemed to be helping us to appreciate one another, and we loved our time together. After about six months, however, that newly found honeymoon stage began to disappear. The anger re-emerged as control.

These were the days of limited, not unlimited, internet on our phones. I will never forget driving to school early one morning when he called as I crossed over a dark and foggy bridge, upset because we had apparently run low on our internet plan. He informed me when he did his search on what types of sites use up the most data the fastest, several dating sites were listed. He then began to berate me about how I was on online dating sites. I was absolutely in shock. I tried to have him explain again because I was so incredibly lost. He accused me of cheating based on low data and a Google search of high use sites. There was no reasoning with him, and the kids were sitting behind me. I told him I would buy more data and that I was done talking. He wasn't. I spent the next ten minutes listening to him yell at me, letting me know he was going to find my profile and prove it. He finally hung up, and I dropped the boys off to their classrooms and then sat in mine, grateful that I had thirty minutes before my students would show up. This would be one of the hundreds of times I would be attacked and/or accused of something crazy. I began to tell him exactly that – you're crazy. But I had no idea this would only intensify as time passed.

While these episodes continued for years, I had no idea these were glimmers into his mental state. I thought he was just an unhappy, jealous jerk. But in the week leading up to his death, I began to realize there had to be something more going on. I noticed him constantly peeking out the front windows like he was watching or waiting for something. I noticed his posture; the fight in him now gone, reflected by his inability to even hold himself upright. I went to say something to him, and he pointed to our Amazon Echo and put a finger up to his lips to quiet me. He mouthed to me that someone was listening. He told me he saw something on his phone through an ad that was targeted at him. All these things crashed into me, and I began to see that he really and truly was mentally disturbed.

After he died, his family made it very clear that this was not a surprise to them. I was floored by these confessions. His brother was the first to tell me this was an ongoing conversation among the family over the years. He then revealed to me that when my husband was younger, he used drugs and was getting into trouble. This trouble is what led to him being medicated at some point. Knowing this, I was transported back to a time when I tried to get him to take things like St. John's Wart or Camu Camu to help with his mental state naturally. I remember him saying to me, "But then I have to admit I have a problem." At the time, I didn't realize what the problem really was.

Another time, in the week before he died, as I brought the remedies up again, he mentioned that he "Didn't like how they made him feel." Of course, I didn't know he was referring to the actual medication a doctor had placed him on years earlier. I had no idea that he had been sick for years. His father echoed these sentiments, stating that he had been fearful of this for so long. His mom went so far as to tell me that he had called her from the ship the year prior, talking about suicide.

All of this was kept from me. I felt so incredibly in the dark. I began to question what I could have done and what I should have seen...and the anger over his death began to surface. WHY did they keep this secret? I told myself that I would have perceived things so much differently had I known. I have no idea if this was true since I was not given that chance, but at the time, it felt so incredibly real to me. I was picking up more puzzle pieces every day.

The night before he died, as I was trying to curb his paranoia, he finally stated, "I need you to hate me." This led to him closing me in my closet and blocking the door as he confessed years and years of wrongdoing and guilt he had been carrying for so long. When he finally released me, I was so angry. I began to do things around the house to keep myself busy while I processed this information. I knew two things. One – I couldn't be married to him anymore. If these things he told me were true, he was not who I thought he was. Two – he needed serious help. This was the first time I really realized there was a problem, though I was still unsure if it was mental illness or if he was just a bad person.

After his death, I was sitting with my counselor in his office at church when he said something that took me by surprise. He said that he suspected my husband was bipolar. At first it did not make sense to me, but the more I reflected on it, the more I realized that this was a very real possibility. I began to research mental illness, specifically bipolar disorder, and saw how his actions could easily be classified and lead to a diagnosis like this. The biggest take-away as I sat in this new information? I began to see that he was in so much pain.

You may hear suicide is a selfish decision. I cannot tell you how many times people would say that to me, and every time I felt like I had been kicked in the gut. I couldn't get over how easily people would toss around their thoughts and opinions on something they had no experience with. Suicide is not selfish. When I think about my husband's mental state that morning – that he was able to grab a gun and make such a decision – it breaks my heart. I cannot imagine the fear and pain that propelled him to end his own life. He wasn't being selfish or trying to hurt us, he just wanted the pain to stop. Once I began to understand that this was pain-driven, I was able to let my anger go and feel relieved that his pain was over. I began to see that he was like a terminally ill patient but without the ability to seek out death with dignity care.

When mental illness struggles are hidden or undiagnosed, it leaves so many questions that impact the survivor's ability to both understand and move forward. These questions can feel like gaping holes in your life, leaving you angry and confused. You will likely also feel some measure of guilt or shame (or both) while you try to process how this could have happened – especially if there was not a mental illness diagnosis. However, take some comfort in knowing whether it was diagnosed or not, to get to this point, your loved one was ill and likely had been for some time. You will continue to find those pieces of understanding as you begin to find more and more clues. As time passes, you will see things from a new perspective. While you might never understand it fully, you will eventually reach some level of understanding that will allow you to let go of the anger, guilt, and shame. I promise.

Four

The Abused Caregiver

When my grandmother went for her cancer screening and found out that the cancer was back and in a much more aggressive way, my grandfather made drastic changes to his life. She retired so she could fight cancer, and he retired so he could take care of her, no matter what may come. I will never forget watching him dote over her. He cleaned, made dinner, took her to her treatments, took her to pick up her wigs, and anything else she needed. She never had to ask. If you were quiet enough, you might even hear him singing to her as he took care of each task. In the blink of an eye, he became a beautiful picture of a devoted caregiver. Very often, caregivers come from within the family to take care of someone who is chronically ill, knowing it is likely their last days. It is arguably the most miserable job title one can hold – even if done with so much love. Even on her worst days, he showed up showing the best of himself.

After eight years of fighting, I remember getting the phone call that she had passed with Grandpa by her side. It was a perfect ending. The man who had loved her for dozens of years and had carried her through was holding her when she took her last breath. I never asked him, but I can only assume he was relieved her suffering was over and she was in the arms of her Savior. And...his job was over. He no longer had to watch her fight and struggle in what was a losing battle. I am sure he felt like he could breathe again – despite his grief – for the first time in years.

Mental illness is just like a chronic illness– except that the physical effects are somewhat unseen. The illness eats away at an otherwise healthy brain, much like a cancer. Some of it can be hidden, but usually, to those that are closest, small signals emerge and multiply over time. Before I knew it, I was an involuntary caregiver for a chronically ill man. But unlike my grandfather, who understood that an illness was to blame, I did not have that clarity. In fact, it would be years before I would realize my job had shifted from wife to caregiver. Even though there was no diagnosis or a treatment plan to follow, I found myself monitoring his mood, social interactions, habits, sleep patterns – the only problem was that I didn't know what any of it meant outside of how it would affect us at home. I used this information to curb *my* behavior, as if I could curb his feelings if I were good enough. I constantly walked on eggshells, testing the temperature of the day and changing course to try to rectify each situation. I had learned to live in a constant state of arousal, waiting for something to go wrong. What I still did not understand was that these were merely the outward symptoms of deeply rooted problems. I did not have a caregiver guide to follow, appointments to keep, medication to administer, or support to help me through it. I was flying blind, not knowing that the dynamic in my relationship was changing drastically with each passing day. I was so quick to justify his behavior due to work stress or where I was falling short instead of recognizing it for what it really was – abuse.

While the outside world saw him as a devoted father, husband, and great at his job, who he was behind closed doors was a different story. It seems he was able to hide his issues at work, but at home he would relax, and we would take the brunt of these behaviors. I began to go to counseling alone to find ways to improve my marriage without acknowledging what was really going on. He would not go with me to counseling but instead agreed that I did need to go alone since I needed to figure out how to be a better wife. I did a great job at outlining our struggles without letting on that there was a deeper issue and instead sought guidance on communication, spending time, listening...all the sticking points in marriage. However, even with his seeming approval, my phone would ring at the end of each session, where he would demand the full details of each word said as he said, "She's a woman, so I'm sure you guys are talking about how I'm the one that's wrong." These phone calls got so accusatory that I eventually stopped going to my sessions. I was at a loss because I had yet to understand that what I was seeking help for was not the problem.

It wasn't until the revelation of his infidelities about two years before his death that I insisted we get marriage counseling. That was where I heard him called out for abusive behavior for the first time. I had put abuse into the category of physical harm, so because I did not have marks, I did not consider what I was going through to be abuse. Because it was not every day, it wasn't abuse. Because we had some good times, it wasn't abuse. But when the counselor detailed how his actions were abuse, I began to see it – the holes punched in walls, the coffee table broken, the screaming and foul language, the threats to find someone better – I saw more of those puzzle pieces scattered throughout our fifteen years of marriage that I was able to pick up to fill in some of the details.

It would be another year or so before I was able to verbalize that what was going on in my home was abuse. It was no longer only directed at me, as he seemed to have a harder time controlling the mood swings and outbursts. The boys began to see and feel this in our home, even though I tried to shield them from it. Not only was the fighting harder to hide, but his frustrations with normal everyday kid behavior seemed to trigger him. There was a time he was upset at the boys for fighting like brothers do – and it resulted in him deliberately breaking one of their toys in front of them to prove his dominance. It also became public – where a mistake made on the ball field led to a string of foul language and speeding out of the ballpark as a show of anger and disappointment. It was no longer just me who was walking on eggshells around him; we all began to live with a man we did not know.

After his death, and the revelation from my therapist about bipolar disorder, I began to see what we went through for what it was. While we will never have a clear diagnosis, it was enough for me to be able to start on my path toward understanding. As I began to research this and other mental health symptoms, it became clear my husband was mentally unstable. My anger for the situation that the boys and I found ourselves in gave way to compassion for the pain that he was in. I finally was able to understand that he was sick, just like any other terminally ill patient, but without any support or treatment to help ease his suffering. The relief that our nightmare was over grew into relief that he was no longer experiencing such incredible pain.

When my father-in-law came to visit one weekend, we were talking about his son's pain, and he echoed these same thoughts. My father-in-law also realized his son was not going to get better and that the best thing for his son was that he was no longer suffering. He also noted that suffering was no longer being inflicted on us, and for that, he was grateful. He found comfort in this as he also grew in his understanding of his son's mental state. For the first time, as I had wrestled with these feelings of relief, having another person within the family draw the same conclusions was incredibly validating and freeing.

I'm aware that very few widows will receive this type of support from any family members. In fact, very often, instead of support there is blame. However, whether you receive this type of external validation or not – your feelings are still valid. Your lived experience cannot be marginalized. While my father-in-law's support meant the world to me, I knew that even without it, I was allowed to be relieved and happy as we moved on with our lives. Very few will understand relief in the wake of suicide, but that does not mean you are not allowed to be relieved that the stress, abuse, and confusion are finally over and there is finally peace in your home.

Part Two: Escaping Rip Currents

Five

I'm Not Mourning Like You

I remember waking up the day after his death and feeling like I had weights attached to my body. I lay there for a long time, replaying the previous day in my head. I questioned my lack of response when he came downstairs and his moving lips when I opened the door. I wondered how we would survive financially. I worried about how this event would damage my kids. I felt the weight of the world holding me down. I knew I needed to shower and try to function, so I sat up in bed. But once I sat up, I couldn't seem to stand up. I sat there, staring at a wall, willing myself to go downstairs. It seemed like forever before I got into the bathroom and turned on the water. I felt utterly exhausted from these actions as I sat on the toilet, waiting for the water to warm. I finally made it in and out of the shower where I wrapped myself in a towel and sat back on the toilet, waiting for the strength to climb back up the stairs. When I finally succeeded, I found myself sitting on the edge of the bed, trying to determine how I would have enough energy to get dressed.

The shock of his loss put me in a place that I did not understand. I was full of questions and responsibilities without answers or the means to take care of things. I was being asked to write an obituary (I never did), plan a funeral, and deal with the never-ending show of people at the house that was about to start. Since he was active-duty military, I also had to report his loss to the command, which resulted in two officers showing up at my door – an image I had only seen on TV. I was so incredibly overwhelmed and utterly lost. Along with the loss, I was also still processing all of the things he had told me before his death. As I did, bits and pieces of those conversations propelled themselves to the front of my mind as I understood them now to be his way of preparing me for what was to come. I began to see how he had planned his death to get through Christmas, to be sure I had his brother's number to contact first, and even how he had already planted into my mind to move into my parents' house – just in case something ever happened.

I found myself repeating, "He's dead," and "He died," and "I'm a widow" as I kept trying to understand my new reality. As my therapist had told me to use clear language when I communicated with the boys, I was trying to do the same thing for myself. I was trying to accept the life that I was now going to be living, ready or not.

I hated that we were not prepared like we were when my grandmother died. With her death, I felt peace immediately – even in the grief. When my grandfather died of a sudden heart attack, it was tough, but I was still able to find peace in the good life he lived and the legacy he left behind. My husband's death was so sudden and violent and full of questions I could not answer, and the peace I was used to finding in death I could not find. This was not a grief that I understood.

While it was hard in the weeks that followed, I noticed that tears were few as we found a new home, went back to work and school, and tried to resume life as normal. That was the phrase that kept being repeated by my oldest – he just wanted to feel normal. I noticed we were making strides towards happiness despite the circumstances. We celebrated my oldest son's birthday – a first "first" without his dad as we began to write a new story.

Overall, we seemed *okay*. People kept asking, and I really meant it when I said we were doing okay. My son had assumed the role of man of the house, and I don't mean that jokingly. He became very concerned about our financial state, wondering how we would afford to pay our bills. As I sat in the kitchen, I began to plan for a completely new life and was tallying each dollar. With a to-do list on one page and a budget on the other, my son came and sat beside me. I tried to tell him he didn't need to worry, but at just ten-years-old, he made it very clear that it was his job to help, because Daddy told him to.

I had to balance the anger in that moment – how dare he put such a burden on his son's shoulders! But I also realized my son's involvement in the planning of our new life would help to calm his anxiety and give him a sense of control. More than once he would ask me if we could afford what we were about to spend, and I understood that this inclusion would not only help him but give me a partner as well. We were learning to lean on each other in our new family dynamic.

My son made a startling realization one day as he sat with me while I made our budget for the month. He said to me, "I am going to miss some things about Daddy. But I am not going to miss the way he acted. He was mean a lot." I often wondered if my son really was okay as he seemed - just picking up and resuming his life. I had expected my boys to cry themselves to sleep for months as they mourned their father's death, but other than small moments here and there, the tears never seemed to overtake them. They never seemed to overtake me, either. When my son verbalized his feelings at the table that morning, I began to realize that we weren't mourning the loss of a husband or a father; we were mourning the loss of a home, a life, plans, and the security of those things. We were all coming to understand our grieving was different than most.

I had a widow friend that I made shortly after our loss. As I watched her grieve, demand answers, pay tribute, and yearn for him – I found myself thinking how incredibly *lucky* she was. How lucky she was to be mourning the loss of the love of her life when I was merely mourning the loss of a style of life. She would think of her husband on special occasions, wishing he was there to share in a moment or a life event that he should have been there for. I would encounter those same moments, glad that he wasn't there to ruin them.

When both of my boys took to the football field as teammates for the first time, I thought, "Man, he would have loved this." But then, almost immediately, I thought, "He would point out each thing the boys did wrong or the coaches did wrong and ruin this for us." I found myself so very glad that I could enjoy this moment without that pain.

It is a very hard place to find yourself in – balancing what you would have liked to have experienced with the reality of what things would have actually looked like. I strongly believe my boys deserve to have their dad in their life, watching them grow up and being a part of each event. However, the duality of that statement is that I also understand their father was sick and abusive, and they would have never had a healthy father standing beside them. That understanding makes me both heartsick over its reality and also grateful they no longer have to experience feeling as if they were not enough. These moments happened repeatedly through the years, and I began to find myself able to rest in the ability to feel the relief of his absence without guilt.

This does not mean I did not love my husband or even that he did not love us. However, I came to realize that the love I had for him had been smothered by years of addiction, secrets, lies, and betrayal. The love and loyalty I had felt at the beginning of our marriage slowly changed and solidified into fear of what might happen if I left. I stayed because the thought of giving up my kids 50% of the time to a man who had become abusive was incomprehensible to me. I felt we would be safer if I stayed and did my best to mitigate the constant storm that lived in our home.

Based on the man I met fifteen years prior; I grieved both the loss of the man I *thought* that he was and who I knew he could be. That man, however, never fully materialized and instead became a man I did not know. Perhaps that was the most painful part – knowing that there was good inside of him. He told me early on that I made him better, but I did not realize that he was using me as a life raft to pull him out of the darkness. The weight of him became too much to bear, exhausting me in the process. Years upon years of being his cheerleader, his therapist, and the only positive influence in our home had turned me into a shell of the person I once was. I was no longer able to keep him afloat, and when that happened, he began to sink down into the darkness that he had been fighting for so many years. I was barely treading water and watching him sink, but his death felt like such a sweet release from the burden of being his caregiver.

These realizations – that I was not grieving him – were a shock to my system. The guilt and shame that I felt was unbearable some days. While I had this talk with one person, it was not something I felt I could share with everyone else. I just knew if I let that piece of information out, which I was desperate to do, I would face a whole new line of questioning.

I began to want to tell my story to anyone who would listen. I wanted them to know about the life that the boys and I had been living for so long. I wanted them to be happy for our fresh start. But that, of course, would invite new questions. The first person I told was my brother-in-law, and it was the first time I had to face the question, "Why didn't you leave?" I was almost at a loss. Why *didn't* I leave? I certainly wanted nothing more than to pick up and leave. As many abuse survivors will tell you, they may not see any clear way out. The fear of retaliation, the threats of taking the kids, leaving you penniless...all these thoughts are incredibly overwhelming and leave you feeling hopeless.

Thankfully, my brother-in-law seemed to understand that this had just not been an option I could see my way through. He seemed to be able to meet me where I was with love and understanding, even in the midst of his own grief. Much like my father-in-law, who understood his son was not going to get better, perhaps he was feeling some measure of relief that his brother's pain was over.

Even in the midst of tragedy, it is okay to be glad in the end result – which is that the pain, the abuse, the nightmare – is over. While there are still days that I am hit with feelings of loss and sadness, it is normal to also feel a sense of relief. You can feel love, brokenness, and freedom at the same time – this grief is messy. It is complicated. It is hard to understand some days. Because your love was complicated, so is your loss.

Six

Shattered and Hopeless

The night before my husband died, I made the decision I could not avoid any longer. I had to leave him. I knew it. He knew it. He was convinced something in his past that had just been made known to me that day was finally coming to get him twenty years later. I had no idea if what he was telling me was even true at this point, but I knew if it was true, the kids and I would be better off without him. There were a lot of things I could forgive and look the other way on, but this was not one of them. He began to talk to me and make plans for his absence. He told me he needed to "take his licks" and would be arrested. His pay would stop. We would be on our own. I kept rolling my eyes and telling him this was not going to happen. Besides, I could not even be sure what he told me was true. I had begun to see that what he *believed* to be true and what was *actually* true was not lining up. Regardless, I got tired of fighting him as he pleaded with me to just "make a plan" so he would feel better. So, that is what I did. I told him if it came down to it, I could sell the house and move in with my parents. I told him they would take us in and help us get back on our feet. He made sure to include that his family would step in to take care of us, too.

Finally, when it was all said and done, he took a deep breath. He seemed relieved that there was a plan. We went to bed, and as I desperately tried to fall asleep, he told me he could never see me move on with someone else. "I know the feeling," I had replied to him. I almost heard the gut punch that this was to him. I think this was where he really saw the pain and the hurt he had inflicted on me for all this time. The next morning's interaction was not much better. Our last interactions and my last words to him haunted me for a long time. Sometimes, they still do.

I cannot even count the number of times that I wondered if my words could have stopped him. If, instead of staying silent and pointing, I had asked him to come sit with me. While my marriage was most certainly over – I wish with everything that is in me that I could have saved my kids from experiencing this type of traumatic loss. I will never have an answer to these questions. I will never know what, or if, there was anything I could have done to make a difference that day. This constant questioning and replaying of these moments in my mind added to the complexity of my grief. How do you process the shock of loss when there   was so much left unsaid and unresolved?

For so many of us who have lost someone to suicide, we are left with these questions. We are unable to really grieve because we are spending so much time in shock and picking ourselves apart in the different ways we failed the person we loved. We blame ourselves for the pain we think we could have stopped. These factors continue to contribute to the immense weight of shame that seems to build with each passing day where there are no answers but instead more questions in its place.

Thankfully, the detective there that day became one of the biggest blessings in my life. That morning, though I could not process it at the time, he told me that someone who is suicidal can very rarely be stopped. He told me once the mind has been made up, it is unlikely to change. He told me even if I *had* stopped him that day, he would have found another day or another method. All he could think about was stopping the pain he was in and the pain he was putting us through. Giving him a pass on his cheating the night before or inviting him to sit with me that morning, ultimately, would not have changed the final outcome. In fact, at one point, someone in his family told me I had "kept him alive longer than he would have been without you." At the time, it felt like a slap in the face – because they knew of his mental health struggles, and I did not – but now it feels like a compliment. As much as I had believed that I was partly to blame, I realized that I had loved him *well*. I was faithful despite the challenges and did far more than others in my place might have done. My job was not to keep him alive but to show him that I loved him and point him toward   Christ. The rest was up to him. He had to save himself.

I began to pick up new puzzle pieces as I continued to process everything, but these pieces were less about him and more about me. I began to take the shattered pieces and hopelessness I had been living in and began to see much of what I was believing was simply not true. As I met with my counselor shortly after one of these realizations, I received confirmation when he said to me, "Amanda-Lee, you loved him well. He knew you loved him more than he deserved to be loved. You need to know that."

I'm not sure why each of these new realizations always seemed to send me off balance – even the good ones. But with each new piece of information, I was beginning to be able to see my marriage for what it was and what it wasn't. After holding myself responsible for his happiness, his mood swings, and his love for so long, I began to see that none of those things were my responsibility. With this fresh perspective, I began to forgive myself for all the things I couldn't see over the years. When I was able to begin forgiving myself, I began to soften towards him and felt a deep heartache for all that he had been fighting alone. It was only at this point that I understood that he had been terminally ill for many years. It was at this point where I began to find hope, pick up the shattered pieces of myself, and began to rebuild.

Seven

The Weight of My (Incorrect) Words

I can't even begin to count the number of times I screwed up in the wake of my husband's suicide. I was so incredibly angry that he would do this to us, and that anger and lack of understanding kept me from saying and doing the right things. I remember, in the initial weeks that followed, telling the boys Daddy had "left us." Even now, looking back at that statement, I am so upset with myself for saying that to my kids.

I didn't even remember saying it until some time later when my son repeated my words back to me. It was at that moment I realized the implications of what I said. That he chose to leave us. That we were not enough for him to stay. That somehow, we were responsible for his actions that day. Along with the loss of their father, I also had asked them to shoulder some of the blame for his death. Because of the abusive language that had become present in our home, you would think I would have been more aware of what my words would convey to my kids. I wasn't. I was so incredibly lost myself; how could I have known any better? I couldn't. I had not yet learned how to handle a situation of this magnitude. So yeah, I screwed up. But I learned to do better.

I know therapy can be extremely scary for adults and even more so for kids. As I continued to meet with my counselor from church, he made it clear that the boys needed to see a specialist for trauma. He gave me a name and a number and made me promise to make an appointment for them. At this point, my kids were still unaware of exactly what had transpired that day. My oldest, however, was showing signs that he knew more than I hoped. While I had only told them their father got hurt and could not be saved – my oldest had asked me if Daddy had hurt himself. I was alarmed. Did he mean he understood it was suicide? Or did he think he hurt himself accidentally?

Either way, I knew I had to be honest with my kids. As we arrived at their first appointment with the therapist, the boys seemed unbothered. First, they were sent into a playroom while I had a quick moment with the therapist. As soon as I was with her, I blurted out that I didn't know how to tell them how he died, but I thought my oldest had an idea. I also knew that if I told one, the other would eventually find out. I was worried about telling my eight-year-old this information. Could he handle it? She agreed that telling them both was probably the best course of action, and we would do it together, and she would help guide our conversation. This conversation was perhaps the most critical conversation I would ever have with my boys; I was so grateful that this time, I had help with my words.

As time continued, and I had more and more of an understanding of what really had been going on in my home, I was able to begin having conversations with the boys about their dad's illness, his actions, and even how the words he used with us were untrue. I was having very grown-up conversations with them, not just because of the content but because I was asking my eight- and ten-year-olds to forgive me for my ignorance. I hated that I needed to bring up a painful topic with them, but I knew that the longer those words sat in their thoughts, the more damage they could do. No longer would we have a home that would inflict damage. I had made mistakes, yes. But I also had the power to correct and heal.

Talking to kids about a loss like this while trying to heal myself was daunting. More than once, I leaned on my counselor and their therapist to help me communicate it in an appropriate and healthy way. There were times they would ask me questions, and I simply did not know the best way to answer. I learned it was okay to say, "I am not sure the best way to answer that. Let me think about it and talk to our friend, and then we can talk about it, okay?" I learned to slow down and seek help. This was not a topic where "winging it" would work.

At first, it was difficult for me to do this. They were opening the door for a conversation, and I was not always equipped to answer them at that moment. I worried that there wouldn't be another "good" time to have that talk. In the end, I got the support I needed to have those conversations. I was able to go back (usually at bedtime when we were doing our cuddles and prayers for bedtime) and bring up the question they had asked me. By then I was better informed on the best way to truthfully answer in a way that was best for them and their healing. Not only did I make sure that I was not causing further harm, but they also learned it was okay to slow down and think about things that were painful. It taught them Mommy was also navigating this path and needed help, and therefore, it was okay for them to get help while they navigated it, too. Just because it happened when they were young does not mean they are not going to have moments as they get older when they will need help navigating. The best thing I could do is to teach them early on that getting proper help is the best course of action.

Much of this applies to talking in general – not just to your kids. It is okay to not answer questions that you aren't ready to answer. There were several times I felt pressured by colleagues to talk about what I was doing in my life as I began to pick up the pieces. There were times I said far too much, and then there were other times I snapped at those around me. Some people asked questions because they just wanted the gossip – and I was so vulnerable and carrying around so much guilt that I desperately wanted to tell the real story. But telling the story to the wrong people only hurt me in the end as it just gave them water-cooler gossip.

There were also people who just could not understand what I was telling them, and I found myself re-explaining myself repeatedly. It was exhausting. I found that these were the people who could not accept the truths I was telling them about my husband – either because it was too hard to accept or they thought I was lying – I'll never know. But I learned to stand my ground, and when it could not be accepted, I walked away. I began to walk away from a lot in my life during this time.

As my life began to pivot in a new direction, I decided not to take those people with me. Not all people will understand or accept what you have gone through. And how can they, if they have not been in this situation themselves? Learn to use your words with those who are truly there to love and support you through this time, and never feel pressured to explain yourself to anyone. It is okay to say that you do not want to discuss something, especially in the early days when you haven't quite figured it all out yet. There were times I had to go back and correct my words – much like I had to do with my boys – and that is so much harder to do with adults.

Much of my growth can be attributed to therapy and counseling. I met with a good friend and pastor for counseling for quite a while. He then encouraged me to seek trauma therapy. I pushed it off for a long time as my concern was the boys, and I thought I was "okay." But after about six months, when the events of that day began to impact my everyday life, so I began to undergo EMDR therapy (Eye Movement Desensitization and Reprocessing). With that therapy, I also was able to talk out some of the situations I found myself in when it came to dealing with people. Much like how I talked to the boys, I learned to slow down and talk it out with someone before I responded. I learned to think through my relationships and if they deserved a response. I learned that my story was mine, and I didn't have to share it with anyone, or I could share it with everyone. I began to understand that my words held weight, and I became so much more careful with how I used them.

Eight

Enduring the (Not-so-Quiet) Whispers

Almost immediately after my husband's death, I was faced with an announcement being sent out to my coworkers. When I saw the email announcing his death and subsequent funeral, I cringed. I had asked to be left alone until the funeral – I could not handle a barrage of calls and texts coming through to my phone. I could only imagine what people were saying. I remember going out to my car so I could sit and have a phone call with my husband's boss as I didn't want the boys to hear what I needed to ask. But as I went outside and saw people milling about, I quickly tried to hide. I didn't want the looks of pity – I know I looked like an absolute mess. I was lucky to shower and get dressed, much less fix my hair and makeup.

After the funeral, we needed to stop by the house to get some things, and I had a similar feeling. I didn't want to see anyone or talk to anyone. I could only imagine what my neighbors – the ones that saw the events of that day unfold – were saying. It wouldn't be long before I found out that everyone had thoughts and opinions on my relationship, my home search, my job, and how I chose to move on.

My husband's death sent shockwaves through the military community. I was shocked by the handful of those who traveled to be there for his funeral and touched by their showing of love and support. Perhaps it was because they knew, deep down, there was a problem. Generally, there were a few sides to him. There was the charismatic, happy, fun leader that some knew. There was the torn and broken person that he tried to hide, but some would tell me later that they saw glimpses of. Then, there were a select few who saw the narcissistic and angry person who felt entitled to whatever he wanted. As the one person who saw all these facets of his personality, it was hard to reconcile what I knew to be true and what I knew to be fake. Especially as people began to talk.

One friend of his had worked with him for many years and had known our family for just as long. Because of this, he saw a little more than most. In some cases, he knew more than me. He validated my feelings by talking about the signs he saw and how he always felt that I could have "done better." He told me he was aware of my husband's addictions, his wandering eye, and his anger, and wondered if I knew.

When others in another state – the ones who knew him as broken – began to talk, it became apparent that his story of brokenness was also a lie. This group began to share their interactions and developed a theory that his suicide was expected because I had been threatening to leave him the whole time they had worked with them. They told everyone I was to blame for his death as he had cried about our marriage to them. Thankfully, this other friend was quick to correct the story, as he knew that I never threatened to leave. Instead, my husband had actually been planning to leave us so he could be with his girlfriend while also engaging with yet another someone on the side. In fact, when it came out that he had given me an STD, I still never threatened to leave him. He was so broken and remorseful that I believed this was the "low" he needed to realize how good he had it. When my friend contacted me to tell me what was being said, I had a panic attack. Finding out what was being said about us was something I had feared, and I was too vulnerable to hear it.

I remember crawling under my covers, wondering how I would ever get through this. I couldn't understand how I had been made the villain in the story – seen as the one who was responsible for taking the boys' father from them. How could people speak about something they were not a part of? However, this is when I found another puzzle piece. His lies and interactions with others were yet another display of his worsening mind. I realized that he truly believed it was all my fault. He told me if he didn't get what he wanted from me, he would find someone else, and by not giving in, it was my fault when he went elsewhere. I realized I would never know the depth of the lies he told me or anyone else. I was going to have to learn to ignore the gossip because I knew what was true in my home.

The next day, I thanked my friend for defending me and explaining how things really were, but I asked him to never tell me again. I told him I was so grateful for his defense, but I was too weak to be able to bear it myself. He promised he would always defend us and would not let these conversations go unanswered, yet would keep them to himself for my sake. I was touched by this act of love for us as I learned I could be in control of how I handled the whispers of those who were desperate for the details.

I continued to be surprised by those who would begin to question each step I took, as if it impacted or threatened them in some way. As I could no longer live in my house, I began to immediately look for a new home. In just a few short days, we had found a new home in which to rebuild our lives.

I was so grateful that the builder was a friend and had just completed it as a spec home days before told me it was mine. However, others wondered why I would dare buy a house so big. Now that there were just three of us, why would I need five bedrooms? Didn't I feel lonely or unsafe? I hadn't yet learned not to reply. I explained that I had sat down with my dad and narrowed it down to the two my builder friend had offered.

One was small and under budget; the other was large and over budget. My dad said to me, "Get the big one. At your age, when you meet someone again, he will likely have kids. You don't need to move the boys again. They need stability. Pick the one that gives you stability and room to grow." He was right – but when I told people all they heard was, "She's buying a big house for her new husband and kids." Cue the talk. One month after his passing and here I was thinking of relationships. Of course, that is not what I was thinking at the time. But it is what people heard.

However, I certainly fueled the fire when, one month after we moved in, I decided to start dating again on the heels of a friend offering to set me up. I agreed simply because I was convinced that I just needed to get the first bad date over with. The other part of me was desperate to find someone to love me the way I had been praying about for so long. I began to think about my oldest, asking me if I would get married again, and his worry over my happiness. With that, I decided to give myself permission to go find it. I was shocked to find it was not a bad date, and I began to wonder if this was the man God had been preparing for me the whole time.

I knew there would be whispers and tried to keep it as quiet as possible. I was so incredibly grateful when COVID shut the world down. When I would go out, I was so worried someone would see me and think it was too soon. I knew they would say so. So, when everyone was forced into their homes, I was no longer worried. COVID dating meant just doing life together – our only outings were to the grocery store to buy chicken and toilet paper.

He came over each day and got to know the boys while they built a raised garden. Then, one day, I posted a picture of us together, enjoying a day on the water. My boys were beaming. It was the same day that my youngest told me that I laughed loudly now and wanted to know why. I decided it was time to stop hiding. It was now three months after my husband's passing, and everyone had opinions.

People at work could not believe that I was dating – and they talked about it amongst themselves. They assumed it was rebound or unhealthy or whatever they determined. Then, I got an email from my boss. Even he decided to chime in since he had "heard" I met someone and detailed why what I was doing was a mistake. Again, I felt a need to defend myself, and I did. I expected there to be some sort of reply telling me he was glad I was doing well or happy. It never came.

It seemed that there was constant, unsolicited chatter on how I should be handling my life. I kept trying to explain how awful my marriage was and how it had been over for some time – which allowed me to move on. I kept waiting to be acknowledged and heard. Where was all the love and support that seemed to show up at the funeral? It seemed that once that was over, they were more interested in getting a full story or some juicy details to share with others. Some just seemed to think I was incapable of making decisions and, therefore, needed instruction and guidance.

People are going to talk – whether you hear it directly or it is relayed to you, there are about to be a lot of comments headed your way if you haven't heard them already. When you are already neck-deep in shame and guilt, these comments are enough to send you straight to bed feeling like you will never recover. It is not easy, navigating all the hurtful gossip while you are trying to heal. It is not easy. But with help, you will make it through.

Nine

Whose Fault Is It?

As soon as he died, I blamed him. I was so angry about what he did to our family. To his family. Most of all, to his own children. I was beginning to connect the dots between his behavior and this outcome. Not only did he end his life, but he preceded it with years of mental, verbal, and emotional abuse. He went down this path and constantly chose to avoid seeking real help until it was far too late. For nearly five years, he cheated on me and constantly made comments that made me feel like I was the problem. My weight and muscle definition became a weekly conversation as a direct result of his girlfriend – a leggy, blonde bodybuilder. Everything from the dinner I made to the boys' sports performance – nothing was good enough for him. I had learned to sweep all of this under the rug to avoid serious fallout – but they now were all bubbling up under the surface. The fallout was now mine to have.

While I immediately felt relief in his absence, I was still left to process not only his death but everything that led up until that point. My anger toward him turned to anger towards myself. How did I end up here? The charming man I met when I was just twenty – whose smile would make his eyes twinkle – was not who I thought he was. I didn't know that just a few years before, he had joined the military to escape his hometown, where he had been involved in situations with women and drugs that should have landed him in jail. I began to understand that I was a life raft, a good girl with a good future, to make him feel like he was a better man. He saw me as a way out of the darkness. One of his family members told me, "We thought he was doing so much better. He met you, and you got married, and he had a good career. We were so proud of him."

I began to understand this was a result of a mental illness that had been around since long before I met him, and I began to place blame on his immediate family. Their admission that this was somewhat expected wrecked me. Another statement that he had mentioned suicide in a phone call just months earlier fueled my anger. How was I the only one in the dark? Why didn't someone warn me or take action? How could they let this happen to his children? Even though I never voiced this blame to them – I would not dare add to the pain they were feeling – I was still angry. My kids were in pain. Even without this vocalization, it cracked an already strained relationship.

I was doing my best to keep my kids as protected and safe as I could as we were back in school and his birthday approached. There was already a plan to go to Disney for a long weekend, and I decided that it should still go forward as planned. I had one caveat. I told his family that they were NOT to bring up the boy's dad unless the boys brought him up first. Immediately upon landing in Orlando, I was met with questions about my request. Why? Did I talk to the therapist? Is she on board with this? Whose idea was this? The real answer was that I knew how my kids were currently doing and I knew how some of their family was doing. I wanted this trip to be light, fun, and carefree. Did I specifically ask the therapist? No. But had the therapist told me to stay aware and open to what the boys may need? Also, yes. Immediately, I was annoyed that I was being questioned as a mother – especially when my only goal was to keep them safe.

My anger from these feelings of blame was starting to surface. When the birthday came and we arrived at the park, the boys were immediately reminded that "Today is Daddy's birthday." I saw a shift in my oldest son. Later he would tell me it ruined his whole day – as we walked around to different rides he would tell me multiple times that he just wanted to get on the plane and go home.

I didn't realize it yet, but what I was doing that day was drawing a boundary. I continued to draw similar boundaries as that first year went on, and they continued to be crossed. Finally, I realized that the continued behavior was reminiscent of what I had endured in my marriage. A lack of respect for boundaries. I began to have anxiety attacks when his family would come to visit. I was still healing from the years of pain, so being thrown into it – even in short bursts – was more than I could handle. My therapist began to help me set new boundaries where I did not have to be present, and yet they could continue to have a relationship with the boys. Over time, the boys began to set their own boundaries with some of their family members as they grew old enough to decide what was best for them.

The family dynamics after his death changed somewhat slowly but continued to evolve over about three years. I was still angry about their lack of communication over his mental health. I began to be angry over the lack of respect for my boundaries. I was even angry as he became idolized as this amazing son, father, and husband – when I knew he wasn't. As I put distance between us, the extended family began to reach out, questioning our actions and informing us of the hurt we were causing. I had so many things I wanted to say - that I wanted to correct. But...simply answered with, "Thank you so much for your prayers." I knew my answers were not ready to be heard and I knew that I was not able to effectively communicate without my own anger.

With therapy, I was able to understand something that I did not understand before. While I had lost a husband, that was different from the boys losing a father and still different from his mom losing a son or his brother losing a brother. The day he died, each one of us lost completely different people. We all held completely unique relationships with him, and not one of us could truly understand the other. Especially since coming to understand mental illness, I can now understand that we will never understand the person that the other one lost. Even with this new knowledge, it was hard for me to see him be celebrated when what I had known for so long was pain. My boundaries became a new part of my life – even though I could see things differently, I knew I could not let myself be surrounded by those who couldn't validate his poor behavior. I grew tired of explaining his abuse and had to learn to let distance and silence be my voice.

It was never my intention to hurt any of his friends or family, but I also knew that being around people who experienced a different, even amazing, side of him was hurtful. Why wasn't I good enough to get that side? I knew it existed, and I saw it years before and had glimpses of it throughout our sixteen years together. But that only made it more difficult to withstand. I continued to wrestle with guilt and blame and wasn't sure when and where I could finally lay that burden down. So, in the meantime, I did what I could to protect myself from further pain. The distance allowed me to keep communication open but without getting too close. It is like watching a flame dance in a fire pit – if you get too close, you eventually get too hot and smell like smoke. I wanted to see it and admire it without feeling the heat.

As I moved on with my life and rebuilt my family, I was able to see that we were all on different paths and different timelines. I finally was able to understand that the only person to blame for his death was him. He had to be the one to want to get help and no single person was responsible for saving him.

It's difficult to navigate when a sick mind gets in the way of getting needed help, but there were plenty of moments of clarity over the years when he was well enough to understand that he was not doing well. Not all of us share that feeling, and that is okay. I am responsible for my own healing, and part of that is knowing when to set down the anger and the blame and move forward without carrying it with me to my next chapter of life.

Ten

How Will I Feel Today?

The healing process is not an easy one. I wish I could say that in a month it won't hurt so much. The path is different for every single person – some will heal faster than others. Some will fall apart daily wondering when it gets better. Others will make it look easy. Because everyone's history, situation, and actual loss event are different, there is no one right way to do this grief thing. Some are healing from losing the love of their lives, and others are healing because they escaped a monster. Some are healing because they are wondering where God was in all of it, and others are healing because they know that God *was* in it. No matter your situation, the torrent of feelings can be all over the place. Some days will be better than others, just as some days will send you back to bed.

I remember being on the phone with a new widow who lost her spouse to suicide. Like me, the relationship had become abusive, and she was beginning to recognize there was a very real mental illness at play. I found it was very cathartic for many women to describe to me the loss of their spouse – down to the very last gruesome detail. At first it was jarring for me, but I realized that they saw me fill a role that no one else in their life could. I was quite literally the only person who shared this experience with them. Not even their therapist truly could understand. I became a sister-in-arms as I was able to hear them tell me about the day that it happened and shoulder the burden with them. This spouse told me the story of that day while feeling anger, outrage, tears, and desperation. She told me she couldn't get a grip on how to feel. She couldn't seem to "sit" in one emotion long before another one would take over. She felt all over the place, and it was exhausting.

I took a deep breath and told her to close her eyes and imagine the beach with an angry ocean. I told her that, right now, she had been thrown into an angry ocean and was fighting a rip current that was taking her out to sea. I told her that for a while, she would feel powerless against the waves as they worked hard to drag her away from the safety of the shore. Eventually, though, she would remember the key to escaping a rip current. Remembering that it is narrow. Upon that realization, she would feel equipped to swim parallel to the shore to break free of its hold.

Of course, breaking free of the current does not mean that you are not still out in the middle of a fierce ocean or far from shore. The waves will still overtake you – but you can now focus on the shoreline. You will continue to make your way into shallower waters and smaller waves. It still exists, and you are still exhausted from working your way in, but you can tell that there is progress being made. Eventually, your feet will find themselves touching the ocean floor, and the water will be under your neck. With each step, still heavy as you fight the pull of each receding wave, you will find more strength to keep you moving forward. Ultimately, you will make it to the surf and turn around to see how far you have come. As the water laps at your feet, you will realize the grief will never fully leave you, but you will have learned how to live with it as a part of who you now are.

As you find yourself in the highs and lows of the emotions that come with working through grief, I cannot stress enough to find help. Whether you have both a church counselor and a trauma therapist or you have a friend who truly understands your type of loss and is willing to sit in it with you – being able to talk openly and process your feelings is vital to improving your own mental state and giving yourself a newfound balance. Life is not going to ever be the same again, and it is going to take some time to find out what life looks like now.

For me, it was essential that I had a counselor at church to help me talk through the questions I had about my own faith resulting from what I went through. My faith was shaken, and I needed to work through this as I rebuilt my worldview. Additionally, I had very real effects from the trauma of discovery and needed a trauma-trained EMDR therapist to help my brain understand the difference between threat and safety. I could not move forward with my life and ignore either of these facets of my life.

There were times when I found myself incredibly angry that God didn't "fix" him. After all, I prayed for years for him to face his demons, speak kind words, and love the family he had. I did everything I could to make him love me. I did everything I could to point him to redemption by showing him unconditional love and forgiveness. And yet...he continued to get worse instead of better.

I understood it had to be his choice, but also understood that God had the power to do it anyway. I couldn't see why he wouldn't intervene and give the boys and me what we needed. The thing was, I found God *was* giving us what we needed. While there was a very real mental illness, I strongly believe much of mental illness is rooted in the spiritual realm. My husband was never willing to admit he needed help – both spiritually and mentally. In fact, this was something he said to me many times over the years as he worsened. It was something he was both aware of and afraid of, and the fear kept him from making positive changes.

As I began to reconcile my spiritual life and feel at peace, I found I was struggling with nightmares, intrusive thoughts, and sometimes physical reactions to certain smells and sounds like gunpowder and the sounds of gunfire from the hunting land nearby. With all the research I had done to understand mental health, I failed to see I was suffering from the effects of PTSD. The nightmares were so vivid that I found myself picturing my husband's dead body as a way to comfort myself that he couldn't hurt us anymore. When these began to become more frequent, I knew my counselor at church was right, and it was time to seek professional help.

Even if you did not have a traumatic experience like I did, it is still possible to suffer from these symptoms after a loved one passes. A friend of mine, who lost her husband to a long cancer fight, also underwent EMDR therapy to help her heal from having a front-row seat to his illness. Now, while I may be a doctor...I am not a therapist. I cannot tell you if EMDR is right for you. I know many people have had amazing results in healing by going through this therapy, but I know it is not without controversy. Some people may need to be put on medication for a while, others may need weekly therapy, or maybe you need dual therapy like me. All that matters is that you take the steps to help you move forward – even if they are just baby steps.

I would be remiss if I failed to also mention how critical it is to take care of your physical state. You may find that due to stress or trauma, you begin to experience physical symptoms you may not have had before. You may see immediate weight gain or weight loss, extreme fatigue, lack of energy, appetite changes, and sleep changes. These are all seen as normal after a loss, but it is important to address them if they become extreme or interfere with everyday life. I know how hard it can be to address your own health, especially when you are caring for children. However, it is important to take care of yourself so you can continue caring for others.

When my husband died, I lost twenty pounds in a matter of two weeks. I knew I had to eat – but I also knew the thought of eating made me want to vomit. I had to make a conscious decision to eat nutrient-dense foods when I did eat instead of wasting it on junk calories. I began to experience problems with my gastrointestinal system as well. I attributed it all to stress and let it go on for nearly two years and only went to see a doctor when it had gotten so bad that it impacted all aspects of my life. I was diagnosed with Celiac Disease, which was not altogether shocking to me. I always knew I had food sensitivities like most people do, but the symptoms had gone beyond irritation. I was shocked to find I developed an allergy in my thirties, but upon further research through the Mayo Clinic, I discovered Celiac Disease can be brought about by severe emotional stress. Through diagnosis and testing, I discovered that I not only had this, but I had also ignored it for so long that it had begun to do serious damage to my intestinal lining. This was my wake-up call. I scheduled an eye appointment, a dentist appointment, a pap smear, and a breast ultrasound as I realized it was time to take care of myself.

In the beginning, emotions are turbulent and hard to predict. You may think you are doing okay, and then all of a sudden, you feel like you are back to day one. Your mind may wander, and you find yourself in a memory rabbit hole that you cannot seem to escape. Or, perhaps that rabbit hole is a sudden revelation as you relive a conversation and realize there was more being said if you had only been able to read between the lines. As painful as these all may be when they happen, just remember that each of these moments also contains the power to heal you a little at a time. Just like a good cry makes you feel better, these moments of remembrance and realization can do the same.

Part Three: Calmer Waters

Eleven

That Is Not Going To Work For Me

As people began to let me down and be intrusive, I was so grateful my counselor friend helped me to understand that boundaries needed to be set. For so many years I had lived in a home where boundaries were not allowed. Countless times, I remember trying to state what I wanted or needed, only to be told that this was not how it worked in marriage. Boundaries did not exist in my home. I had learned to give way to his whims, his moods, his anger, and his will. My counselor saw this behavior was beginning to translate into my new life. I did not understand that boundaries were not set to keep people out but instead are set to keep ourselves protected and safe. Additionally, they can actually help to *strengthen* relationships. By showing respect and love for another, you demonstrate you are a safe place. Unfortunately, that was missing in my home, and if I was not careful, history would repeat itself.

In my marriage, he had clear boundaries. His phone was off-limits, he had set up a separate bank account I did not have access to, and had expectations in the bedroom. If I dared to cross him on any of these issues, there was hell to pay. I didn't want to see his phone or his bank account as I knew only hurt would meet me there. But the bedroom? I refused to meet those expectations. He made me well aware of what would happen if I did not comply, and he followed through.

Emotional boundaries were also ignored. If he was ready for a fight and I was at work or with the boys, he did not care. He wanted it to happen when he was ready. I would ask him to wait, but what I wanted was immediately dismissed. Over the years, he cared less and less about my well-being, so much so that I eventually dismissed it myself. As a caregiver, the only people's well-being that I cared about was his and the boys'.

As I forged a new path forward, I began to sacrifice myself once again for those around me. For their needs. For their desires. They became what was most important. After all, weren't they suffering too? Didn't they lose someone also? I was the one who was glad he was gone – so, therefore, it was my job to bend to everyone's will. But after a few months, I took my counselor's advice and began to craft boundaries for myself and my children.

When it was time to hold the military service, several months later, due to COVID, I was given a clear set of limits due to the constraints set forth by the CDC. I was given a date and told there could only be a handful of people present. I was going to have to choose which of his family would get to attend the service. I couldn't imagine being put in a worse spot. Finally, I sat down with the boys, letting them know we would be making our way to Arlington to bury their father in just days. Both let me know they didn't want to do this. They knew how hard this was going to be, even harder than the funeral. I told them that, essentially, we would have to go alone, as we were limited by who we could bring. I wanted my parents to be there, as I needed their support. I knew his parents and brother should be there, but all three of them could not make it due to our limited numbers.

Finally, I talked to the boys about how they wanted to do this. It was their dad, and much like the funeral itself – they were in charge. What they asked me for surprised me. They said they didn't want *any* of our family there. Instead, they wanted some friends of ours to attend. These friends were also a family of three, left behind after *their* dad had passed just a few years before. They needed to be with people who understood *their* loss instead of having to be strong for the audience. Thankfully, our friends didn't even hesitate and made the drive with us, stayed overnight, and supported us as we watched the flag fold for the last time and placed his ashes into the niche.

It was an awful day. Our seats were even placed several feet apart, far enough so I could not even reach my boys as the tears poured down their masked faces. I was so grateful for my friend who ignored the rules and stepped forward to place a hand of support on their shoulders. As we drove away, conquering the last awful thing we had to do, I knew I did the right thing by letting them choose. However, when I let his family know shortly thereafter, I was met with confusion, anger, and hurt. I had to draw a boundary that protected the boys, honored their wishes, and hurt people at the same time.

The intention was never to hurt anyone, and I tried to explain the restrictions (which I later found had been slightly lifted the day of his final placement and would have allowed everyone to come) we were under. Instead, we were questioned as to why we could be so cruel. This was a very difficult season for our family of three as we navigated how to heal while also causing pain. Sometimes boundaries cause pain and sometimes that is what prevents us from holding to them.

Many people have a hard time with boundaries, especially when they are used to being in control. They see boundaries as roadblocks to what *they* want instead of honoring what someone else might need. My therapist helped me to see that boundaries would help to mitigate problems, especially following the hurt that was caused by his burial and the events that followed. She explained to me that I could explain what we needed, "Please don't bring up their Dad unless they do," and then make changes to relationships based on the responses to these requests. As the boundaries were crossed, I knew I had to draw a firm line in the sand. This became the first large crack that began to strain relationships.

I recognized that these visits were setting back my own healing and had to step away from these times. I finally understood that I did not have to be in charge of or a part of those relationships and merely coordinated their time together. After some time, however, the boys began to express their frustration at my ability to set a boundary while not allowing them to do the same.

What the boys didn't see, however, were the times that I explained myself and my decisions in an attempt to find mutual understanding and respect. I also had to explain to the boys that we simply don't cut people out of our lives without reason, and we make sure that we explain it to them in an attempt to explain our feelings and reasons. This puts the responsibility on the other person – knowing they are now making the decision whether or not to honor your boundaries. The boys and I got to the point where I would no longer speak for them. I instructed them that they were in charge of their boundaries with one rule – they had to be honest without being intentionally hurtful. Both boys had these conversations, and it led to a drastically different experience for both of them. One decided to spend time with them; the other decided not to.

I absolutely hated this. I hated seeing my youngest so angry at people who love him, yet I understood he was hurting. People often forget the pain that exists for the one who *sets* the boundary. We don't relish locking people out or hurting them. I wish for nothing more than for us to all be together in the wake of such heartache and tragedy. I so wish we could understand each other. I wish I could see the amazing person they remember, and I wish they could understand the man he had become.

But, until that happens, I will do my best to set clear expectations, walk away when they are not met, and support my boys as they learn to navigate the same. Nobody talks about the grief you feel in having to stand firm on a decision, knowing it is not what you want to happen, but you know it is what you and your kids need. These boundaries are needed for healing but also add another layer to the already-complicated grief you are experiencing.

After years of being with someone who did not care about my own well-being, this became my number one concern as I created my new life. I walked away from a job I loved because the lines between personal and professional were far too blurry. I walked away from friendships. I needed distance between myself and so many things – just so I could think and plan and do without everyone offering advice on how I should act. How long should I be single? How often should I be in therapy? How thin I had become (Eat a cheeseburger! They'd say.)

It was just too much. Even though I knew much of it came from a place of love, I needed the distance and the time to think and decide for myself.

If you have not set boundaries for yourself before and you start now, especially after a loss, people are going to have strong opinions on it. They may be offended or even hurt – especially if they are just trying to help. That's okay. They are allowed to be offended and hurt, and you can still set those boundaries. You can explain your reasons and feelings and why you need this, and they may not understand. They may even think you are crazy or make you a topic of conversation. That might have been the hardest part for me. The gossip. I wanted to seek it out so I could correct the story, but ultimately, you cannot control what anyone else does or thinks about you. If you are recovering from abuse like I was, it is extremely hard to stand up for yourself when it is something you haven't done before. It took me a whole year before I began to walk away from things or people who were not supportive.

At first, setting these boundaries can feel incredibly lonely. And while I cut my "friends" list way back (both on social media and in-person relationships), I found the opposite to be true. My smaller group became the loudest cheerleaders and the best hype squad I could have ever imagined. God sent new friends to replace the ones I had to walk away from. In my case, cutting back led to an increase, making my life rich and abundantly full.

While very often people interpret boundaries to be created to keep people out, what people fail to understand is setting boundaries is an act of self-care. As you grieve and heal from your loss, there is a shift in what you are able to handle. As you begin to create a new life, oftentimes from scratch, it can be incredibly overwhelming to know where to start first. For a time, you may find you have to say "no" to anything that is not necessary. Learning to say no can be a hard first boundary to set, especially if you have been saying yes for so long to make others happy.

I know for me, no was not an option for so many years that it was difficult for me to learn how to say it. Some people may be surprised when you begin to do this somewhat "out of character" response. Remember, saying no has nothing to do with what is begin asked, and instead has everything to do with cutting out anything that will overwhelm you as you try to refocus and make necessary decisions.

Safeguarding your personal spaces, be it physical or emotional, is the next step to setting boundaries. As your body recovers from loss, you may find yourself tired, short-tempered, and easily stressed. By taking steps to safeguard your spaces, you eliminate the need to "always be on" and allow your body to rest, reflect, and recover. Perhaps this means you take your work email off your phone – safeguarding your time outside of your nine to five to focus on being home with your family or taking time to care for your body on a walk or at the gym. Whatever it is, your mind cannot recover if you do not give it the space to do so.

Saying no and safeguarding spaces cannot happen without being assertive. Being assertive does not mean you are rude or unkind, though the word can have a negative connotation. Much like I told my boys, they had to communicate without the intention to hurt others, and we must also communicate clearly using truth and kindness. For many of us, especially if you have been unable to do this in the past, this can be difficult when you are used to apologizing or bending to placate another's feelings. Just remember, express what you need in clear and concise language without being negative – and you do not have to justify it unless you want to. Simply stating, "I am unable to make that work this weekend," communicates your answer without apologizing or being negative. Sometimes, less is more.

Remember to get support. I know for me, I needed permission in the beginning to set boundaries for myself. I remember sitting with my therapist, explaining the feelings I had around some people and why. Without judgement, she gave me the tools I needed to express what I needed, "This weekend does not work for us," which morphed into, "We will let you know of a good time," and eventually, "We are only able to make this work during this time." I learned that beyond saying no, I was able to then set a boundary for when it *could* happen, as well as allowing me to make the decision as to when I was able to tolerate it.

Remember that, for many, this is a learning process. Boundaries are not always easy to set and you may need some practice and confidence before you are able to successfully set them. Give yourself grace as you learn this new practice and remember the endgame, your own mental well-being and healing.

Twelve

Give Yourself Grace

I can't even count all the ways I screwed up as I navigated this new life. I let myself down, I let my kids down, I let my job down, and I let my (and his) family down. As I designed a new way of doing things for myself, I found that I was constantly at odds with what the "old me" would have done. I was evolving into a new person, and it was like I was learning to be an adult, a mother, a daughter, and an employee all over again. I wasn't necessarily doing any of them wrong, but I did things differently than before, which, to some, looked like I was messing up. And, of course, at times, I was.

As I learned more about suicide, I realized that my uneducated self spoke incorrectly. As I learned more about how to move on, I didn't always do it with the best intentions. As I learned how to set boundaries, I hurt people in the process. As I learned how to be a single parent, I forgot to seek advice. As I learned how to be a working mom, I realized I had to commit to less.

It was around this time that I discovered the Grit and Grace Project, a women's ministry that I have been so honored to be a part of for several years now. Combining both the idea of giving grace to myself while demonstrating grit spoke new life into me. I could be both a screw-up and a powerhouse at the same time. "Grace gives kindness to ourselves and others even when it's hard. Grit determines that life challenges will not defeat or define us."

For some reason, I had always applied the idea of grace as something I give to others – but give to myself? That was something I hadn't considered before. For the first time, I realized that while I gave grace and understood that I received grace, I had yet to give and receive it from myself.

I began to stop beating myself up for all the mistakes I had made in previous years. Whether I should have known something deeper was going on, or I should have left when I found out he was cheating, or I should have protected my kids better from the things going on in our home...it no longer mattered. This was where I was standing now. I may have been standing on a pile of rubble, but I was still standing. It was up to me to decide how I would go forward. I could sit on that pile and rake myself over the coals about all the ways I messed up. I could think about how horribly I had allowed my kids to be traumatized. I could sink into a puddle of despair and self-destruction as I focused on all the wrong things. Or, I could learn to give myself grace on what I didn't know then.

With all my anger at myself and then his family over how he died, I could have stopped there. I could have stayed angry and spent time blaming every person possible for the situation I found myself in. As much as I wanted to do that in the early days, I knew I couldn't let that happen. I hadn't necessarily found the ability to give grace to myself yet, but I knew I had to keep moving, one foot in front of the other.

As I shifted my focus to all of the things I had to get done, it allowed me to stop circling around this feeling of anger. Were there still days where I was ticked off? Absolutely. The first time I tried to go to the gym after his death, I barely got checked in before I lost it and had to leave. All I could think about was how I didn't measure up to his body builder girlfriend. How I would never measure up. But then, my son looked at me and said, "It's okay, Mommy. We tried. We'll try again another day."

Did he really know why the gym was so hard for me? No, but he didn't need to. All he knew was that I needed a little grace. His comment quickly sobered me up. He was right. Today wasn't the day; we *would* try again another day. With my mindset changed, I didn't focus on how I didn't make it into the gym that day. Instead, I focused on the fact that I tried. This became one of the first exercises in giving myself the grace that I deserved.

Even when I was getting it right, I found that I needed to still apply some grace here and there. As I made the right decisions for the boys and myself, I continued to be questioned over many things. As we prepared to move, I knew I would need a new set of furniture for my bedroom. Then, as we headed to the furniture store, I decided I would be getting new furniture for the boys, too. After all, they were using their nursery convertible furniture, and while it was solid, it had seen better days. Off to the store we went, buying three new bedrooms of furniture. The boys thought it was so much fun as I told them to go pick out what they wanted for their new rooms. I loved seeing them happy and dreaming of our new life in our new home, but it was still so bittersweet. I remember walking through the store thinking, it is not supposed to be this way.

Upon getting back and scheduling our movers, I decided all the furniture left behind was going to be put on Facebook Marketplace, for free. I wanted nothing to come with us from our old life into our new one. It was an odd moment, posting furniture I had so lovingly picked out with their dad by my side. I kept thinking, if you had told me that day where this furniture would end up – I would have told you that you were crazy.

As I sought out help to pack up and settle into our new place, people couldn't believe I had just gotten rid of so much stuff and bought new. Was that a wise way to spend my money? In those moments, I learned to apply grace. I had to believe that it came from a place of love, and if not, did it matter? Giving grace to myself and those around me was probably one of the biggest steps in my healing journey. By accepting that the only person I could control was me made it that much easier to keep giving grace.

Was it always that easy? No. There are some people who I still struggle with when it comes to grace and forgiveness due to the hurt of their actions and words. So, while I have been unable to give them grace just yet, I have been able to give it to myself as I work on giving it to them.

Perhaps the hardest part of grace was accepting it when it came to how my kids were hurt throughout all of it. Of course, the initial event and my words surrounding it were awful, but in time I was able to correct those with my kids. However, when I began to see, through little glimpses of conversations with my boys, that they had been impacted far more than I thought, it destroyed me. Being kind to myself when I felt I had ruined them for life was simply out of the question. I really thought I had shielded them from his actions and his words by making excuses or ushering them out of the room. I thought their young minds would easily forget abusive language and harsh treatment. Imagine my surprise when I would be tucking them in at night, and one of them would mention, "Was Daddy sick that day at the ball field when he sped off yelling?" or, "Was it the sickness that made him scream at me and break my toy?" or, "Did he really mean it when he said he didn't need you?" Yes. I was absolutely wrecked by each of these questions. What kind of mother was I to let my sons think we were we were the reason for his behavior? With each new contemplative question at bedtime, I realized my babies were doing exactly what I had been doing. Revisiting each scene in their minds, picking it apart and analyzing it with new knowledge.

They had a hard time processing what mental illness was, especially because he did not look sick. I remember trying to explain it to them like a cancer. Their grandmother had fought breast cancer and lost her hair as a result. I told them we could see Memaw's hair had fallen out because she was sick, but Daddy's sickness was inside his brain, so we couldn't see the pieces that were falling out. We had many more discussions about his illness, and as we did so, they revisited more and more of those terrifying scenes as the weeks went on.

Of all that I went through, this was the lowest of all my lows. I couldn't fix this. I couldn't undo it. I was so thankful when my therapist said to me, "All we can do is the best that we can with the knowledge that we had at the time. You had very limited knowledge then. How could you have done any more?" She was helping me to find grace for myself once again.

As I kept moving forward, I had a choice to make. I could let this event, those years of abuse, defeat and define who I was. Or, I could decide to pick myself up and power through with grit and grace. It was not always easy. There were times when I would feel like a complete failure as a wife, a daughter-in-law, and a mother. But as I gave myself grace and sought help when I felt I could not do it on my own, I began to understand that I truly did my best. I was not going to let this cloud hang over us any longer. I was going to keep going, and I wasn't just going to survive it. I was going to *thrive.*

Thirteen

Restoration Will Come

*A*ـ*fter you have suffered a little while, the God of all grace, who has called you to his eternal glory in Christ, will himself restore, confirm, strengthen, and establish you.*

1 Peter 5:10 (ESV)

I remember coming across this verse one day shortly after I had found out about his first affair in 2017. The affair had already gone on for two years, and I had no proof it was physical. They both claimed it was emotional and was now over. I knew better, but without proof, I felt there was nothing that I could do. When my phone rang that day, and *her* husband was on the other line telling me he discovered a text message between my husband and his wife – we were both devastated. I remember talking to him as I sat in my office, hearing how utterly defeated he sounded.

We were both incredibly broken by the betrayal, but we decided that we would move forward in our marriages and do our best to keep our families intact. So when I scrolled past this verse one day, I felt God was talking to me. I just knew that he was working. Of course, he was going to restore our marriage. I remember looking up the word restore in its original language, Greek, to find out exactly what was meant by that. What I found was that restore meant to "make better than their current or former state." Not only would my marriage get better, but I just knew it was going to be better than it ever was, according to this verse.

Instead, things got much worse. Two years later, he came home one day to tell me he had given me an STD. I had never felt more humiliated than I did that day when I had to go see my OB/GYN for a full STD panel. As I sat there in my paper gown, my doctor walked in, "I know people. You say the word. I will make sure he pays for this." He was joking, of course, and honestly, I was so grateful for it. I wasn't sure how to even talk about this, how to admit I had been cheated on, and now *this*. My doctor let me know that he understood my pain and was trying to help shoulder it with me. As he finished the exam and sent the nurse in for bloodwork, I found myself getting dressed and wondering who was looking back at me in the mirror. Who was *that* girl? How could my life keep getting so much worse? Where was the promise of restoration?

As I waited for clean test results, my husband sunk into depression. And instead of worrying about me, I began to spend all of my time trying to make *him* feel better. I stopped feeling sorry for myself and instead found that I felt bad for him because clearly, he was so distraught about what he had done to me. To us. Within a few weeks' time, I was given the all-clear and the remorseful man that had been around vanished. We began to fight about everything, and very often, I was blamed for his behavior. I constantly heard where I needed to be a better wife and was questioned about who I was seeing and what I was doing at all times. He was easily provoked, and even the boys began to see his temper flare over insignificant things.

A few months later, I received a phone call from *her*. She had finally seen the angry man I knew and wanted to break things off. He was angry and threatening, and she called to tell me she wanted him to leave her alone. She told me they had been in love; her own husband was abusive. She began by confiding in him as a friend and before she knew it, she was in love with my husband. But as it progressed, he became jealous and possessive. She even told me at one point, he had told her he would kill himself if she left him. I had no idea what to even say. In fact, while I know I said things to her, I could not even tell you how the rest of the conversation went. Sometimes, your body hides things you don't want to remember. I know I got off the phone, packed up my boys, and took them to a friend's house with little explanation other than, "I need you to stay the night here tonight."

At first, he was angry at me – I guess because I found out directly from her. His only focus at this point was how awful she was and how this was all her fault. But then, a shift. He became the husband I always knew he could be. Thoughtful, caring, loving. He even became one of the coaches for my son's baseball team, realized his harsh treatment of our older son was damaging, and began to coach the way a dad should. Unfortunately, my older son saw his younger brother was getting the dad he deserved and wondered why he didn't deserve that. As the months continued, things were going well until I expressed concern that his former girlfriend's family would soon be moving to our area on orders. What if we saw them? How would that go? This conversation sparked him trying to contact her again under the guise of alleviating my anxiety.

One month before he died, I received a text from *her husband*. This time, he was threatening me. All he said was, "I warned him." As I called and begged and pleaded with him not to take action, to think of me and the boys, he wanted to know if I was really going to stick around. Why wasn't I leaving him?

This was the beginning of the end. My husband began to have paranoid thoughts – thinking his girlfriend's husband was trolling him or people were keeping an eye on him. He got a message stating he was going to NCIS (Naval Criminal Investigative Service). He thought a secret (one that I wasn't aware of yet) he told his girlfriend was being weaponized against him. This crime he committed years earlier was finally going to take him down. I finally began to realize something was seriously wrong with him. He even said as much and would say that he wished he would get some sort of diagnosis or a reason for why he did the things he did. While remorse had always been a show before, I began to see genuine remorse over the life that he had been living and the people he hurt in the process. As it came crashing down on him, he could no longer bear the weight of his sins.

A few months after his death, a friend of mine was at a brewery with her husband and some of his friends. One of these friends had seen us together the week before and asked about me. She immediately told him I was unavailable. He told her that was fine. He would wait.

As she relayed this to me, I chuckled and rolled my eyes. He was awfully confident, wasn't he? Everyone had given me their thoughts and opinions about how and when I should proceed with my life, including that I should not date for one year. Why one year? I have no idea, but I thought that one year sounded like a good plan. I like plans. I like control, especially when I feel so unsettled. But as I sat in Florida on our first trip after his death, texting back and forth with some male friends that I had known for a long time, the flirting started. And boy, did I feel ALIVE. I desperately wanted to feel that way again.

As I returned home, I texted my friend who was at the brewery that night and told her, "I'm tired of living like this. It's time I start dating, and I should at least get the first bad date out of the way." I asked her some questions about her friend and gave my permission to hand out my number. The very next morning, he sent me a message. The minute we started talking, I *knew* something different was afoot.

Is it normal to start dating again so soon after such trauma and loss? No. At least, I don't think so. All the widows I knew at this point had lost spouses due to illness or accident, and they lost the love of their lives. They needed so much more time to process and get to a place where they felt they could even consider loving someone else. I didn't have that type of loss. My marriage had been over for more than five years, and I had already been in therapy for much of that time trying to heal. Sometimes, I was so jealous of my friends who lost someone they loved so much. Their grief was normal. Mine...wasn't.

I was so grateful when COVID shut down the world. As I grappled with dating and everyone's opinions, COVID allowed us to hide from the world. We spent every single day together – his family and mine – as we navigated it all together.

As I became aware that my husband had likely suffered from bipolar disorder and found out this new man in my life had an ex-wife who also suffered from the same, I felt God was intricately weaving our broken pieces together. We were both cheated on, devastated by betrayal, and forced to raise our children while trying to protect them from the ugliness. As I had nightmares and panic attacks, I would call him in the middle of the night, and he would talk to me until I was calm again. As my boys struggled with their feelings, he was able to talk to them about his own Dad and the abuse that went on in his home growing up. There were so many parallels that were present in our new relationship that there was no doubt in my mind that this was divinely appointed.

I struggled, however, as I watched other friends try to find love again and fail. Why was I so blessed so early? Why was I given this chance? I felt so guilty for my happiness. Even years later, as I met a good friend for dinner, I posed that same question to her. Why me? Why did he fulfill this so fast for me while I watched others struggle? How do I proclaim his faithfulness to me while it seems to go unanswered for others?

She pointed out that my new family had emerged out of years of waiting. Mine was waiting within my marriage, and he was waiting after the divorce. We both had to wait for the other to be ready – and he told me that months before we met, he had given up. He had told his daughter he was done. That he couldn't go through that again and he refused to do that to her again. There was so much pain for years before it was finally our time.

I was reminded of all the years I had been praying. God had directed me specifically in those dark years to pray for the husband I deserved, a new house, a new neighborhood, and neighbors...it all came full circle for me in that conversation. He wasn't fixing someone who wouldn't accept help, and he was delivering exactly what I had been asking for for so many years. He was just giving it to me in a different package.

I have watched my children be taken care of by complete strangers from organizations that care for military kids. I have seen them grow in their understanding of their father to the point where, while they miss him, they will tell you their life is better than it was before, and they are so grateful for that. This is extremely bittersweet as they acknowledge who we knew him to be – as I wish I could have protected them better – but knowing they appreciate the life we have now is extremely beautiful.

I firmly believe restoration always comes…though it may not come in the package we imagined. I fully believed God would change my husband, but he cannot change someone who isn't willing to change. He knew that, but I didn't. In all of my anger and confusion I began to see an entirely new life emerge as I saw prayer after prayer be answered right before my eyes. Not only was my family restored, but it was also made better than it was before by being granted a man who adored me and the boys and gifting me with a new daughter.

While we had struggled financially due to his lifestyle, I saw financial burdens lifted and financial security left in its place. My dream of furthering my education was granted. He didn't give me what I asked for. He gave me what he saw fit, and it was so much better than I ever could have expected. I can't say when you will see those promises fulfilled, but I can tell you that restoration is promised. Remain faithful in the waiting.

Fourteen

What's Next?

There is this idea that has been circling around on social media – the idea that 41 in the Bible signifies God's deliverance from something. When a friend of mine posted a quote from a book centered around this concept, I found myself inspired and began investigating the number 41. As I did the research, I saw that it was true. We all know that it rained for 40 days and 40 nights before the rain ceased. We know that the Israelites walked for 40 years before they finally walked into the promised land. Jesus himself fasted and was tempted in the desert for 40 days before the devil fled.

There are dozens of instances of how things went terribly wrong, before day (or year) 41 finally showed up. Dozens of podcasts, sermons, devotionals, and books have been written on the idea that life can be awful – but there is better coming. The more I studied this, the more I saw it as such a powerful testament to remaining faithful. It can be overwhelming, trying to map out a new life, new goals, new ideas...all on your own. You may be asking yourself, "What's next?" every single day as you both mourn the life you had planned and attempt to create a new one from scratch. It's not always easy and can often be overwhelming.

I am very type A, or at least I used to be until I went through this. Once the funeral was over, I found myself sitting at my parents' house that night, thinking about what was next. While I had a laundry list of things to do, I sat down, pulled out the notes app on my phone, and began to make a list of all the non-negotiables I wanted in my next partner. I knew that no matter what my plans were if I didn't make clear lines in the sand over this, it might derail everything else I would set out to accomplish.

I had already settled in my first marriage due to being young and naïve, and I was not going to make the same mistake again. Twenty-three specific points later, I closed my list and shifted my focus to all the immediate needs in my life. I made budgets, completed paperwork, made dozens of phone calls, created a new will, bought a new house, sold a house...I worked towards stability in my new reality. I watched God provide as social security, which should have taken three months to take effect, happened in just two. I was given a home to live in before I even closed, and I had people reach out and help with packing, moving, putting up blinds and TVs, and even storing some of my things in transition. It was both a very hard time and so incredibly beautiful.

As things began to settle and the pandemic hit, I found myself grateful to be home where I could really think about what was next. I had so many dreams I had put aside or forgotten about as I just wasn't in a position to make them happen. As all the roadblocks cleared and I no longer had someone to answer to, I began to revisit them. I had always dreamed of two things: owning a little place at the beach, where I always felt the most peaceful, and going back to school to get my doctorate. Both had been not just denied but almost ridiculed over the years until I finally stopped daring to dream. I began to investigate property ownership, and with the drop in the market due to the pandemic, my dream was turning into a reality.

As I brought it up to my boyfriend, I was shocked to see him light up with excitement for me. I had never experienced the joy, support, and love of a partner like that before. However, as I realized what I could afford would be a 1986 special with *original* carpets and appliances...I began to think this wouldn't be possible. He offered to go look with me, and he carefully took stock of the place that I had really focused on, room by room. I nervously waited for his assessment. When he said, "I think we can do this. It's all cosmetic," I thought he was crazy.

It was bad. It was a complete gut job. But, as we added up the cost of the renovations, we decided to give it a go. We spent that pandemic summer creating a beautiful condo with the best sunset views. And, while my plan had just been to have a little slice of paradise, I dipped my toe into the vacation rental market and found success. Turning something so ugly into something so beautiful with my own hands was incredibly satisfying, and so healing for my soul. I was able to create beauty out of the mess of my past.

As a new in-person school year began and I fell into a new routine, I found myself admiring myself and what I had accomplished over the summer. With that boost of confidence, I came across an ad for a graduate program. It was the same program that I had applied to and been accepted into just four years prior but had to decline due to a lack of support from my late husband. I marinated on it for a while and, again, approached my boyfriend and asked his thoughts about it. Not only did he support this idea, but told me he would do whatever I needed him to do to make it happen.

I researched the program again with a fresh perspective and purpose. Just months later, I was working towards achieving my next dream. Only three and a half years after I suddenly became a single mother, I walked across the stage in disbelief as a doctor. As I approached my program director to be hooded in the ceremony, I asked him, "How did you get me here?" as I was so thankful for his support and guidance. His response shocked me; "How did I get you here?" he said, "I got you here by getting out of your way. You did this yourself."

While we all move through grief and heartbreak and guilt and anger with (hopefully) people around us to support us through it, ultimately, we have to do this for ourselves. Some of us will have an easier time of it than others, some of us will fight different battles on our path to healing and some paths are longer or bumpier than others. No matter the path, it is up to us to determine what is next in our lives. I could give credit to a boyfriend or a professor for my success, but neither did the work for me. It certainly was easier with the support of the right people by my side, but that doesn't mean there weren't times that I wasn't crying over a statistics class or missing a kid's sport or a dinner because of a choice I made. At one point, I simply could not work full time and go to school full time, and I stepped away from my job to adjust my focus. While I knew it was the right choice, it also was incredibly painful.

Starting with small tasks may be the right start for you if you are feeling nervous or fearful about trying something new or stepping out of your comfort zone. Accomplishing smaller tasks is a great confidence builder as you learn to navigate life on your own. In time, you may start to think about bigger goals or things you want to accomplish. Maybe you want to go back to school and finish that degree. Even if it seems daunting, take some time and explore the options available to you. Even if you decide not to pursue it right now, you are still exploring possibilities. Even thinking about what steps you might want to take next can be difficult or overwhelming and take time to process. You may find success or even failure as you move forward on some of your ideas. Failure is okay! Sometimes, failure is just learning what wasn't right for you.

I know of several friends who attempted to find love again after a death or divorce and just couldn't seem to find the one. One in particular was deeply hurt when a relationship ended, but she also was able to see that she was settling. In the absence of the relationship, she was able to see that she had seen some red flags but had not fully accepted them until it had ended. She realized that this relationship hadn't been right for a while but was grateful for the courage she had had to even try to find love again. Of course, she struggled at first with what went wrong, but she was also able to see the new lessons learned in the midst of it.

For others, it may mean a change of job or a neighborhood – if nothing else, but for a change of scenery to leave the old memories behind. Maybe what is next for you is a fresh start in a new place with new people. I once had a widow whom I worked with pick up and move to a completely different country with her kids! Everyone's what's next will look different. This can be challenging when people question the steps you are taking in your life – I know that mine certainly were! Not all of them work out, and some may see that as a failure, but all of it is a lesson learned that will further equip you for your *next* next.

With all things, be sure to find balance as you begin to take steps forward. If you have known me anytime in the last ten years, you will know that I have a hard time sitting still. I like to constantly move on to the next thing, sometimes before I have even finished what I am working towards. I didn't used to be that way. However, after years and years of abuse and belittling, I find that achievement makes me feel both valuable and validated. I was constantly told my job was not good enough since I chose to work in non-profits; I was told I was a failure as a wife; I was mocked about getting my doctorate. I felt so small for so long that I began craving some new trophy that I could hold as validation as a person.

Even now, I am still learning what it means to be content and happy with where I am. I am starting to accept that I don't need more achievements to validate who I am in my career or in my home. After I obtained my doctorate, I looked ahead to a new career and was disappointed to find that finding a new job was not happening quickly. A year later, as I worked two part-time jobs, I began to see I was content with my current workload and what I was doing. It allowed me complete flexibility to schedule and use my days as I saw fit. Instead of working full-time, I was able to use my days writing this book, going to the gym, and spending time running kids all over the place. I realized I didn't need my *next* next to be a title. I no longer felt the need to validate my existence with achievements. So, as you begin to move forward and heal, remember to do the things that make you happy. After years of seeking validation from my spouse, I realized that the only person I needed to please...was me.

Keep moving forward in both big and small ways. As you begin to craft a new life for yourself, take some time to write out your biggest and forgotten dreams. Is there a trip that you always wanted to take? Take it. Is there a degree you want? Go after it. Do you want to move to a new town and start fresh? Go for it. Are you ready to find love again? It's worth it. Do you want to enjoy the life you have without restrictions? Sounds amazing to me.

Fifteen

For the Military Spouse

I f you lost your partner to suicide and they were in the military, there is an entirely different level of grief and anger to contend with. My husband always refused help, as he was convinced that he would be pushed out for mental instability. Even with more and more suicides happening each day in the armed forces, there is little effective help. Depending on which study and which branch, suicide is seen as either the leading cause of death or the second leading cause of death. First or second, it is far too high. When it got really bad, I insisted he get help. He did so through Military One Source, which advertises confidential help. He went every two weeks, and I tried really hard not to ask him about it. But on the occasions I felt that I could ask, I often felt lost and helpless and confused after. Not that he would say too much, but on more than one occasion he told me, "I just need to know what is wrong with me. Why do I do the things that I do?" Sometimes, these memories bring me comfort because they tell me that these were moments of clarity – where he realized that he was doing and causing harm. I was able to believe in these moments; he wanted to get better.

As things progressively got worse, he saw his command flight surgeon for help. The surgeon put in for a referral for mental health services, and that referral would come nearly *six weeks later* when he was no longer thinking clearly enough to seek help. Around this time, just days before his death, I went through his wallet to try to find the business card for the therapist he had been seeing. I looked him up, and what I found left my mind swirling. This practice had a Google rating of 1.8. I read review after review that said things like, "I'm not being listened to," "terrible attitudes," and "lack of caring." It was clear that these life-saving, confidential services were not adequate. As he spiraled in the twenty-four hours before his death, it was clear that I needed to do something. But as it was Christmas, my plan was to call the next day to try to get him help. Even with this spiral, I never thought he would have taken his life.

My anger towards the government continued for many months. While I was grateful they took good care of us in the weeks after, I began to think more and more about the terrible care and the six-week wait fora real mental health referral. At one point, I took the business card and the referral letter to a lawyer friend of mine, and he called another lawyer who had some experience in these situations. As I pulled out the business card of the therapist, the lawyer said, "Whoa. He's not even a doctor. He wasn't getting proper help because he wasn't seeing the right person."

It was like a kick in the gut. As I told our story, I told him that my husband's behavior had finally pushed me to the point of leaving him, but my boys deserved to have a dad. If he had gotten proper care, there was at least a chance he could have gotten the right help so that my boys would not have had to go through all this pain. The lawyer told me we had a case, but I had to be okay with becoming the poster child for suicide loss in the military community. I wanted to be that person. I wanted to make noise and enact change, but could I bear that burden? Could I put the boys through that? Ultimately, I decided I could not go through with it, but I was also angry at myself for not being brave enough to do so.

Suicide loss in the military, though it makes the news all over the country, is still extremely stigmatized. Some spouses will be granted survivor benefits, and others will not – and as far as I can tell, there is no rhyme or reason to who qualifies and who does not. Because most do not have a diagnosed condition (due to inadequate care), it becomes hard to prove they had a mental health condition due to their service. It is a catch-22. They need a diagnosis for proper help, but they are afraid to seek help due to what a diagnosis could mean. Some are medically discharged as they are found unfit for service, meaning they can no longer provide for their families. If they are lucky, they are able to prove a diagnosis from service through the VA and receive disability, but this is another hard program to navigate. So many are denied every single day and are wasting time and energy fighting for the benefits they deserve. Others seek help, like my husband, and receive inadequate care or are forced to wait too long for a proper referral that comes too late. I know others who have had a family member commit them to a VA hospital when they have become a danger to themselves, but they are simply turned back out on their own later without proper help. I have one friend whose son has been in and out of the VA hospitals at least three times. He has contacted state government officials and still has not gotten help for his son.

In 2018, the Army's 82nd Airborne enacted a new policy on memorials, excluding all suicide deaths to restricted final honors. It was a slap in the face to all of our service members and their families. It sought to invalidate post-traumatic stress and traumatic brain injuries – both of which often go undiagnosed. Instead, policies like this inflict more shame over the cause of death and significantly impact a family's ability to heal. Military policies regarding suicide can sometimes seem illogical. I cannot explain why some get full burial rights and others do not. I'll never understand why some families are left out in the cold while others are well taken care of. It adds to my anger towards the military, and some of the blame for my husband's death rests solely with them.

With all of the shame that comes with suicide loss, even when civilians notice the news is filled with the problem, it is hard to admit that is how your loved one died. While my husband did so many things wrong, one thing I feel strongly about is that he was a good sailor, and I have tried to impress upon my kids that their dad is *still* a military hero. How he died does not undo his service to our country, and they are allowed to still be proud of that. Even still, it is so hard to talk about. People have asked me, "Oh, he died in combat?" or "Did he die in an accident?" In the past, there were times when I have just said yes...simply because I don't want him to lose the respect that his service deserves. However, in time, as I faced these questions from a place of healing, I began to change how I phrased his death. Just yesterday, as I sat at the doctor with my son, filling out medical history for our family, it asked for his cause of death. My answer was simply, "PTSD." Even without an official diagnosis, this allows his death to present with some dignity to whoever may read the file. Suicide is still so stigmatized, but PTSD commands honor and respect.

The people we lose to suicide in the military deserve to be remembered for the good they did in that uniform. We may never know the battle wounds their brain collected over the years, but we know them to be very real. These battle wounds may be invisible to the eye, but we certainly all experienced their impact behind closed doors. Regardless, your loved one is still an American Hero. Your children deserve to know and love the person they were in that uniform, even with all of the wreckage they may have caused at home.

I suspect my husband suffered from mental health issues from before the military, but they were certainly amplified when under the stress of deployments, serving in combat, working on flight decks, not being home to watch the kids grow up, feeling like a failure as a husband, being told to man up when he couldn't anymore, and putting up with hostile treatment when he tried to get help. Each of these is a mental wound that so many of us could never imagine.

At the same time, military families are faced with losing an entire way of life and a culture they have grown to love so much. Within months families are forced to move off-base and find themselves juggling a new ID that doesn't quite identify them as Active Duty but also not-quite retired. The AD-Dec qualifier is one that will need explaining over and over again, sometimes even on base. As I recently renewed my ID, I was rudely told I couldn't renew my ID without my husband present or a form with his signature on it. If I hadn't been so far from my loss, I am sure I would have lost it. I was just so grateful my boys were not present as I looked her directly in the eyes and said, "Look at my ID. Tell me, what status is my husband?" Her superior walked into the room as I informed her he was deceased, something she should have immediately seen along with the military death certificate I handed over.

The amount of times I have had to inform someone that he is deceased is sickening. All the doctor's bills for the boys are addressed to him, and the boys hate to see them. It is awful having to explain over and over that he is gone, yet everything for them is in his name. We are never sure where we fit, within the military or separated from it.

I will never forget when, days after his death, as I sat with our casualty assistance officer, he informed me I could not remarry before fifty-five. At the time, I just stared at him; how could he even talk about that right now? But as time moved on and I fell in love with a man who loved me and my boys as if he had always been meant to, I realized how ridiculous this was. It is an archaic rule that passes ownership of a fallen family to someone new and lets the government off the hook financially. Thankfully, many people are working hard to remove this rule and give so many families back the benefits they lost when they dared to fall in love again. The average age of a military widow is *just twenty-two*. Being told you cannot move forward, especially when young children are involved in simply cruel and unusual. And yet, it is an ugly part of our lives.

Being a military spouse grappling with suicide loss has so many more facets and layers of loss, anger, frustration, and even humiliation that no more of us should ever have to deal with. Even still, be proud of your American Hero. Do not let others marginalize or stigmatize your loss. Be their voice and allow them to be remembered for their service instead of their death.

Sixteen

Never the Same, But Full of Hope

Going through any type of trauma, whether it be suicide loss, terminal illness, or any type of abuse, will forever change who you are. The person you used to be has undergone a dramatic change through the new knowledge you have gained about yourself as a result. Perhaps you learned things about your partner, have a new understanding of mental illness, have done the hard work of healing, or even lost friends and family. Life, as you know, looks drastically different than it did before – and that is scary. I wish I could say you will "get over it" and go back to a normal life. The pain will go away. The triggers stop. You'll forget that old identity. You won't. The images of the day my husband died will forever be etched in my mind. The month of December will always be a strange mix of Christmas excitement and dread. Some years will be easier than others, but that is grief. It ebbs and flows, sometimes lapping at your feet and sometimes feeling like it is going to take you under.

As crazy as it may sound, I don't regret one moment of the pain that turned me into who I am today. Of course there are things I wish I could change, but the person I am now is so radically different than I used to be. Fear, trepidation, low self-confidence, and missing self-worth have been replaced with fearlessness, boldness, confidence, and pride. For the first time in my life, I know who I am, and I am so proud of myself for having the faith to walk through the fire that was before me.

The guilt and shame are easy to carry. It makes sense to blame yourself, even as a victim of abuse. But as long as we carry it, we cannot grow and develop and develop into who we were truly meant to become. I don't know your story, but I know mine, and it is ugly. There is so much I didn't unpack on these pages that would just serve as further proof of the restoration that has happened in my life.

I mentioned the original Greek for the word restore in 1 Peter 5:10 meant "to make better than it was before," and how I thought that had to do with fixing my marriage. He didn't. Instead, he did me one better and gave me something that was so much better than I even prayed for. Then, He used all I had been through in order to forge a completely new career path with a new focus on helping others through trauma. He took all the things I forgot that I even wanted to do and made them a part of my new life. Remember that he told me to pray over my neighbors? He gave me the BEST. He knew what was coming my way and had been preparing me for about two years before that fateful day even happened.

When I was working in suicide widow support with TAPS, I began to encounter a lot of physical violence stories from those whom I talked to. Some were murder-suicide attempts; some might have been, but they left before the suicide happened. As I kept coming across these stories, I was brought back to when I was praying for my safety. More than one time, I was scared of him. There were times I hid all weapons in the house "just in case." The fact that the boys and I are still alive is not lost on me. When he told me the night before he died, "I can't bear to see you with anyone else," that could have been a warning. People who aren't in their right mind do awful things. This realization drove me to a new level of appreciation for the life I had been given.

My boys hear me say it all the time, "You take every opportunity that you are given." There have been foundations that have reached out to offer my kids incredible experiences, and when they hesitate, I always tell them to do it. Always try something new. You may fail, but at least you failed trying! My oldest started learning to fly a plane at just thirteen-years-old. He recently asked me to tag along on a flight where he was 100% responsible for landing the plane on his own – which he says he hates because it is the most stressful part – he touched down, greased it as he likes to say, and the smile that spread across his face was so rewarding.

When I decided to go after my doctorate, I certainly didn't think I could do it. However, being given a scholarship, I would not allow an opportunity like this to pass me by. As I walked that stage, I was so overcome by pride in myself and the abilities God had given me, in part because of all I had been through. The last fifteen years of my life have taught me so much more than I ever could have imagined, but I was open to learning everything I could about what I went through, why I went through it, and how to grow from it as a person.

Some of us will take longer than others to pick up enough of the pieces left behind to make meaning of what has happened in our lives. It will take time to forgive ourselves and those around us. But that time, understanding, and grace will develop into the grit we need to move forward as a better version of who we used to be. Not just that, but I hope as I leave the pile of rubble of my former life behind me, I can help others do the same.

The other day, I saw some cardinals (those ruby stars in violet skies)—one turned to the other bird & dropped a seed into its mouth – one after the other, after the other. & when the world wheels on pain & teeters on uncertainty, a tiny crumb, a tiny gift, a tiny seed, a fragment of hope under this small blanket of stars – it can never be too small.
-Anne Sparow[1]

---

1. Anne Sparow, Inspire by Anne Sparow (Blurb, 2021)

Questions for Processing

C hapter 1

1. Take this space to tell your story without worrying if it is too much, too graphic, too raw for others to handle. Tell it how you see it, and don't let other people's thoughts and perceptions get in the way.

_____

_____

_____

_____

_____

_____

_____

_____

_____

_____

_____

_____

_____

_____

_____

_____

Chapter 2

1. Have you discovered any secrets in the wake of your loss? What were they? How have you worked through them?

_____

_____

_____

_____

_____

_____

_____

_____

_____

_____

_____

_____

_____

_____

_____

_____

_____

_____

_____

_____

_____

_____

_____

Chapter 3

1. Take some time to research mental illness. Between this chapter and what you researched, what are you beginning to understand now that you did not before?

_____

_____

_____

_____

_____

_____

_____

_____

_____

_____

_____

_____

_____

_____

_____

_____

_____

_____

_____

_____

_____

_____

_____

2. As you reflect over the life that you shared together, are there any red flags that you are beginning to see now that you didn't before? As you continue to heal and move further from your loss, revisit this section and continue to write these down as you understand more about this loss.

_____

_____

_____

_____

_____

_____

_____

_____

_____

_____

_____

_____

_____

_____

_____

_____

_____

_____

_____

_____

_____

_____

_____

_____

_____

Chapter 4

1. At any point, either before or after their death, did you feel over-burdened? Drained? Unappreciated? Abused? Not enough? Take the time to write down any feelings that you experienced before their death.

_____

_____

_____

_____

_____

_____

_____

_____

_____

_____

_____

_____

_____

_____

_____

_____

_____

_____

_____

_____

_____

_____

_____

_____

_____

2. After their death, did you feel a sense of relief? A burden lifted? Thankful that their pain was over? Thankful that your pain was over? In what ways?

_____

_____

_____

_____

_____

_____

_____

_____

_____

_____

_____

_____

_____

_____

_____

_____

_____

_____

_____

_____

_____

_____

_____

3. Do you feel that you have to keep your feelings to yourself, either because of guilt or other's inability to understand?

_____

_____

_____

_____

_____

_____

_____

_____

_____

_____

_____

_____

_____

_____

_____

_____

_____

_____

_____

_____

_____

_____

_____

Chapter 5

1. What do you miss most about the person that you lost? Is it the person themselves? Or the loss of a marriage? The loss of a life plan? The loss of what you knew it could have been? The loss of yourself throughout it all?

_____

_____

_____

_____

_____

_____

_____

_____

_____

_____

_____

_____

_____

_____

_____

_____

_____

_____

_____

_____

_____

_____

Chapter 6

1. Are you struggling with the last words that you spoke? If so, what do you wish you could have said last instead?

_____

_____

_____

_____

_____

_____

_____

_____

_____

_____

_____

_____

_____

_____

_____

_____

_____

_____

_____

_____

_____

_____

_____

2. Perhaps you weren't the perfect spouse or partner; but it is important to remember that none of us are. If you said things out of anger or hurt, you are still allowed to have and express those feelings. Remember, *we can only do the best we can with the knowledge that we had at the time*. In what ways can you allow yourself grace to forgive yourself for what you didn't know?

_____

_____

_____

_____

_____

_____

_____

_____

_____

_____

_____

_____

_____

_____

_____

_____

_____

_____

_____

_____

_____

_____

Chapter 7

1. In what ways do you feel that you failed the person you lost?

_____

_____

_____

_____

_____

_____

_____

_____

_____

_____

_____

_____

_____

_____

_____

_____

_____

_____

_____

_____

_____

_____

_____

_____

2. Were you in a delicate space at the time of their passing (divorce, separation, a fight, alcoholism, cheating, etc) that makes it feel more difficult?

_____

_____

_____

_____

_____

_____

_____

_____

_____

_____

_____

_____

_____

_____

_____

_____

_____

_____

_____

_____

_____

_____

_____

_____

_____

3. In what ways do you *know* that you did *not* fail the person you lost. Remember, we can only do the best we can with the information we had at the time.

_____

_____

_____

_____

_____

_____

_____

_____

_____

_____

_____

_____

_____

_____

_____

_____

_____

_____

_____

_____

_____

_____

_____

_____

_____

Chapter 8

1. What are some things you said that you look back on now and realize were untrue?

_____

_____

_____

_____

_____

_____

_____

_____

_____

_____

_____

_____

_____

_____

_____

_____

_____

_____

_____

_____

_____

_____

_____

2. It is okay to make mistakes in the wake of loss; what are some mistakes that you made as you tried to understand the world around you?

_____

_____

_____

_____

_____

_____

_____

_____

_____

_____

_____

_____

_____

_____

_____

_____

_____

_____

_____

_____

_____

_____

_____

_____

_____

Chapter 9

1. What are ways people have spoken to you or about you that have been
   hurtful?

_____

_____

_____

_____

_____

_____

_____

_____

_____

_____

_____

_____

_____

_____

_____

_____

_____

_____

_____

_____

_____

_____

_____

2. Are these people important to you? If not, do they matter in the grand scheme of things? If so, can you talk to them about the hurtful words?

_____

_____

_____

_____

_____

_____

_____

_____

_____

_____

_____

_____

_____

_____

_____

_____

_____

_____

_____

_____

_____

_____

_____

_____

_____

Chapter 10

1. What emotion do you find yourself struggling with most? Anger? Hurt? Confusion? If it is anger, have you been able to express it to someone? Even if it is the person you lost? If you are hurt by their actions (or the actions of others during this loss), have you been able to tell them why you are so hurt?

_____

_____

_____

_____

_____

_____

_____

_____

_____

_____

_____

_____

_____

_____

_____

_____

_____

_____

_____

_____

_____

_____

_____

_____

_____

2. If you have been unable to really express these emotions, I would encourage you to write a letter detailing how this loss has impacted you. Like my spouse on the phone, don't be afraid to get out every detail. In doing this, you may feel that these emotions will be less likely to overwhelm you.

Chapter 11

1. In what ways might you need to set a boundary?

_____

_____

_____

_____

_____

_____

_____

_____

_____

_____

_____

_____

_____

_____

_____

_____

_____

_____

_____

_____

_____

_____

_____

2. What stops you from enforcing a boundary?

_____

_____

_____

_____

_____

_____

_____

_____

_____

_____

_____

_____

_____

_____

_____

_____

_____

_____

_____

_____

_____

3. What things do you need to say "no" to?

_____

_____

_____

_____

_____

_____

_____

_____

_____

_____

_____

_____

_____

_____

_____

_____

_____

_____

_____

_____

_____

_____

4. What spaces do you need to safeguard?

_____

_____

_____

_____

_____

_____

_____

_____

_____

_____

_____

_____

_____

_____

_____

_____

_____

_____

_____

_____

_____

5. Practice some ways you can use assertive language to communicate your needs.

_____

_____

_____

_____

_____

_____

_____

_____

_____

_____

_____

_____

_____

_____

_____

_____

_____

_____

_____

_____

_____

_____

_____

_____

6. Who do you have that can help support you through boundary setting?

_____

_____

_____

_____

_____

_____

_____

_____

_____

_____

_____

_____

_____

_____

_____

_____

_____

_____

_____

_____

_____

_____

_____

Chapter 12

1. Do you feel that you deserve grace for not knowing what you didn't know? Why?

_____

_____

_____

_____

_____

_____

_____

_____

_____

_____

_____

_____

_____

_____

_____

_____

_____

_____

_____

_____

_____

_____

_____

_____

2. Grace is giving yourself or someone else, "undeserved favor." It can be hard to extend this to ourselves, especially as you battle guilt. If you are struggling with guilt, what are some small ways you can begin to show yourself grace?

Chapter 13

1. What mistakes have you made, either before or after your loss?

_____

_____

_____

_____

_____

_____

_____

_____

_____

_____

_____

_____

_____

_____

_____

_____

_____

_____

_____

_____

_____

_____

_____

_____

2. As we begin to forgive ourselves for our mistakes, we begin to regain the control that we lost. In what ways can you begin to forgive yourself for your mistakes so that you are able to begin moving forward?

_____

_____

_____

_____

_____

_____

_____

_____

_____

_____

_____

_____

_____

_____

_____

_____

_____

_____

_____

_____

_____

Chapter 14

1. Take some time to journal all your hopes and dreams and ideas. Just because they are in writing doesn't mean you have to go through with any of them. Take the time to think and dream as you begin to figure out what's next. Sometimes we need to put it all out there and then marinate on it a while and come back to it. I would challenge you to come back to it in a couple of weeks, or months, and see where you find yourself leaning. Do you want to pursue any of the things that you wrote down? Do you have new ideas to add?

Resources

There are dozens of organizations available if you know where to look, but these are the ones I found the most helpful, prominent, and important ones that you need to know.

1. *Tragedy Assistance Programs for Survivors (TAPS)*

TAPS is a national nonprofit organization providing compassionate care and comprehensive resources for all those grieving the death of a military or veteran loved one. What I love about TAPS is that they directly provide help in a myriad of ways. They will help find you therapy help guide you through difficult tasks such as military benefits, the VA department, and education benefits. Additionally, they have suicide postvention programming, children's and young adult support, and monthly seminars and care groups both online and in-person.

Contact: 24-hour Helpline: 800-959-TAPS

2. *Social Security Survivors Benefits*

Social Security survivors' benefits are paid to widows, widowers, and dependents of eligible workers. This benefit is particularly important for young families with children.

Social Security was a godsend to me in the early days. Thankfully, a widow-friend pointed me to them just days after my husband's passing. I had no idea they had monthly survivor benefits to help me care for my children as we lost my husband's paycheck. File immediately as it takes a few months for all the paperwork to process.

www.ssa.gov/benefits/survivors

3. *Grief Share*

Grief Share is a national grief support group with chapters across the country. This 13-week program helps you learn how to cope and receive support along the way.

www.griefshare.org

Acknowledgements

Boys, thank you for letting me share our ugly story so that others can see the beauty that came come from the ashes – because really – our life is so incredibly beautiful now, isn't it?

To the love of my life and those who walked beside us as we picked up the pieces, thank you for supporting me as I seek to help others, even if it is sometimes uncomfortable.

About the Author

When my husband died, I found myself hiding inside the house, worried about what everyone was saying about me. Whenever I ventured out, I would hear bits and pieces of what people said, what they thought happened, why he did it, and how I should have prevented it or at least seen it coming. There were times I felt compelled to correct people and to tell them what really happened, what *had* been happening for years. Other times, I didn't have the energy to fight them. I was seeing both a counselor at church and a therapist specializing in trauma recovery, but it was still so incredibly difficult. I was handed half a dozen books on how to be a widow...how to grieve...how to cope. I would pick up each one and flip through it, only to realize each time that the author had no idea what I was going through. I wasn't the typical grieving widow.

After a while, I quit my job as a teacher and began to work for an organization called Tragedy Assistance Programs for Survivors. I was put on the survivor care team, and I was exclusively providing support for spouses of suicide loss. I was desperate to make meaning of what I had gone through, but what I didn't realize was that these women would give me a deeper understanding of what it means to be a suicided widow. What I found was that our stories were eerily similar. My guess is that 75% of the women I talked to detailed ugly stories of abuse, addiction, and mental illness that had gone undiagnosed in the months and years before their spouse's death. More than that? We all felt some degree of relief that the world we had been surviving in for so long was finally over.

I went back to school to earn my doctorate in educational psychology after realizing the profound impact that this had on my kids as they made their way through school. With a focus on childhood trauma, I engrossed myself in research and found that there was a lack of support in the school system for these kids – and their teachers. After I obtained my doctorate, I continued my studies and earned a certification in Trauma Informed Educational Practice, focusing on trauma within the military community. Although I have made the shift from working in survivor care to focusing my efforts on support within the classroom, I know that there is a lack of resources out there for survivors of suicide loss. It is time that changed. No more widows should have to walk this path feeling alone, ill-equipped, or full of shame. I am hoping that this book becomes a light to guide you in the darkness.

This book is for:

- Those who have lost a spouse or partner to suicide loss

- Those who have lost a spouse or partner to any loss where you were their caregiver

- Those who have endured abuse

- Those who know someone who has lost someone to suicide

- Those who need to see that redemption and restoration are possible even in the darkest of times